Richard III

The King in the Car Park

A Medieval Game of Thrones

Neil Mackenzie

Copyright © Neil Mackenzie 2014

The moral right of the author has been asserted.

Apart from any fair dealing for the purpose of research or private study, or criticism or review, as permitted under the Copyright, Designs and Patents Act 1988, this publication may only be reproduced, stored or transmitted in any form or by any means with the prior permission in writing of the author, or in the case of reprographic reproduction in accordance with the terms of licences issued by the Copyright Licensing Agency. Enquiries concerning reproduction outside these terms should be sent to the author

ISBN: 978-1492316626

Note

This book is intended for those new or relatively new to the study of the controversies surrounding Richard III. I hope that it will provide not only an insight into this fascinating king but also the impetus for those whose interest is stirred to embark upon the study of the huge range of books and materials devoted to him.

For the sake of clarity, after Richard and George become the Dukes of Gloucester and Clarence respectively, I refer to George to by his title, while Richard is still referred to as Richard.

CONTENTS

Names

Simplified Family Trees

1	The King in a Car Park?	1
2	The Charge Against Richard	3
3	Richard's Early Life	8
4	Appearance and Character	69
5	The Road to the Throne	84
6	King Richard	115
7	Governing the Kingdom	146
8	Invasion and the Battle of Bosworth	161
9	The King in the Car Park	171
	Appendix	177
	Notes	183
	Select Bibliography	189
	Index	191

Names

The number of people in this history possessing the same christian names may cause a little confusion. The list below and the family trees may prove helpful in clarifying matters by showing most of the principal characters.

Edward IV	son of Richard Duke of York, brother to Richard III, Clarence and Edmund
Edward V	son of Edward IV, one of the Princes in the Tower
Edward of Lancaster	Prince of Wales, son of Henry VI
Edward, Prince of Wales	son of Richard III
Edward, Earl of Warwick	son of Clarence and nephew to Richard III
Edward Woodville	brother of Elizabeth Woodville
Richard III	Duke of Gloucester, son of Richard Duke of York, brother to Edward IV, Clarence and Edmund
Richard, Duke of York	father of Richard III, Edward IV, Clarence and Edmund
Richard, Duke of York	son of Edward IV, one of the Princes in the Tower
Margaret Beaufort	mother of Henry VII
Margaret of York	sister of Richard III, Edward IV, Clarence and Edmund, married to the Duke of Burgundy
Queen Margaret	Margaret of Anjou, wife of Henry VI
Elixabeth Woodville	married to Edward IV
Elizabeth of York	daughter of Edward IV, sister to the Princes in the Tower, married to Henry VII
Elizabeth of York	daughter of Richard, Duke of York, sister to Richard III, Edward IV, Clarence and Edmund

Richard III
Simplified Family Tree

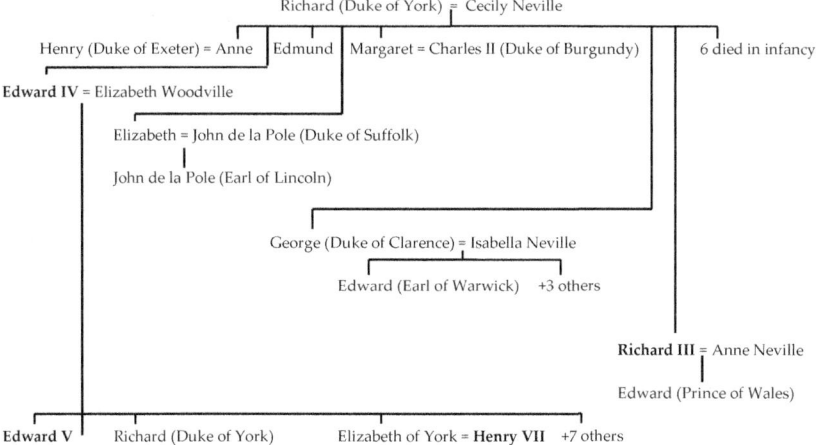

Henry VII
Simplified Family Tree

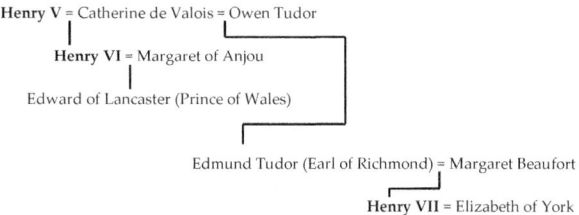

-1-

The King in a Car Park?

The excavation begins

It is an irony of history that following the chaos of Reformation and the destruction of the religious houses of England, Richard, a king whose reputation was made into a monument of notoriety, lacked a monument indicating his resting place. There was no grave around which admirers could gather or mourn, regretting the death of the last Plantagenet, no sepulchre for detractors to disdain or scorn, considering medieval England well-rid of a murderous tyrant. It is not inappropriate that mystery surrounded the site of Richard's burial, for mystery surrounds the life of this most-maligned king, a life that is still bedevilled with controversy. Was Richard the wicked hunchback, who, in cynically plotting his path to the throne and securing his crown, summarily executed his friend Hastings, manufactured evidence of the illegitimacy of the boy king Edward V and his brother prior to having them murdered in secret, and so far disrupted the good government of the realm that he provoked a rebellion led by the Duke of Buckingham before the successful invasion of Henry Tudor finally brought peace to a land suffering under the ruthless sceptre of this bloody-handed tyrant? Certainly this is the opinion of many, yet Richard's life and reign defy easy explanation or judgement. And there are those who not only regard the most serious charges against Richard as unproven but argue that given a longer reign he would have gained renown as one of England's greatest kings. That the range of evidence is able to support such contrary positions gives a clear indication of the enigmas that lie at the heart of this history.

Recent archaeological excavations offered the hope that at least some of the mysteries surrounding King Richard might be resolved. Historians, who had been able to trace the history of the friary of Greyfriars in Leicester, had suspected for sometime that the body of Richard might lie beneath council buildings or in the car park. Yet typically, there was no certainty even of this, for there was a rumour of longstanding that at the destruction of the monasteries the body of Richard, having been disinterred, had been flung into the River Soar. Moreover, the size of the site, the impossibility of excavating beneath the existing buildings, doubts over whether the skeleton had decomposed and the difficulties of identifying any bones as Richard's - should any indeed be found - made such an excavation an unappealing project.

However, unattractive as such a venture might have been, the persistence of Philippa Langley eventually secured funds for a limited excavation of the car park, although the archaeologists entertained little hope that they could unearth the long-lost skeleton. Langley's conviction that Richard's body lay beneath the car park was strengthened by an unscientific hunch, for in 2009 she reported feeling freezing cold as she passed a particular spot in the car park. Returning to the car park later she remarked on the strange coincidence that in the meantime an *R* for *Reserved* had been painted on the space adjacent to where she had sensed so strongly the presence of England's long-lost king.

On the first day of the excavation, leg bones which suggested an undisturbed burial were discovered. Could this skeleton, surviving against all the odds, be that of Richard III?

-2-

The Charges Against Richard

The devils of history hold us in their grip. We are fascinated by their cruelty and their cunning, are shocked by their excesses, and yet yearn to understand them. It is easy to feel the safe thrill of vicarious dread at mention of their names and deeds; and so it is hard to admit that some of our devils may in fact lack the stench of sulphur. Often with reluctance do we allow our images of them to slip, finally accepting that what had so fascinated us is but a paper villain inked in black, while the real figure lurks at the edge of our sight, disappointingly neither better nor worse than most men. Richard III is one of history's favourite devils: Shakespeare's *"villain"*, *"bottled spider"*, *"poisonous hunchbacked toad"*; the *"Monster...enough for many ages"* of Richard Baker; and, in the words of the statute demanded by Henry VII, the king guilty of the *"shedding of infants' blood"*. Many have been captivated by the large, malevolent shadow that Richard has sometimes seemed to cast over the end of the English Middle Ages and it would seem to be a disappointing anticlimax if he were, after all, simply a king of his time, maybe even an admirable one.

The charges against Richard can be summarised. His small dark physically misshapen body with a hunched back and possibly withered arm marked the outward manifestation of the evil that lurked within. In his determination to seize the throne by ruthlessness and cunning he was prepared to let no one stand in his way. The son of the Duke of York, he was acquainted with the violence and vicissitudes of the Wars of the Roses, for as a child he learned of the death of his elder brother, Edmund, at the Battle of Wakefield, and how this was avenged by his eldest brother, later King Edward IV, at the Battle of Towton. Richard was created Duke of Gloucester and until Edward produced an heir was the second in line to the throne. However, when the first in line to the throne, his brother Clarence, conspired with Warwick to reinstate Henry VI, Richard sought safety with his brother Edward on the continent. Returning with Edward he fought in Edward's successful campaign at the Battles of Barnet and Tewkesbury. After the Battle of Tewkesbury he murdered Henry VI's son, the Prince of Wales, by stabbing him, and oversaw the execution of other prisoners. As a man aptly suited for the task, he was given the commission to execute Henry VI in the Tower.

However, although laden with land and honours, Richard's ambition was thwarted when Edward produced two sons. Furthermore, Clarence, forgiven for his treachery by Edward, married Warwick's eldest daughter. Richard's avarice prompted a vicious row with Clarence when, to lay claim to a portion of Warwick's lands, he married another of Warwick's daughters, Anne Neville, whose husband, Edward of Lancaster, Prince of Wales, he had illegally executed after the Battle of Tewkesbury.

When Edward finally responded to the danger posed by Clarence, Richard, under the cloak of friendship, and mindful that his brother's death would bring him closer to the throne, plotted against him and gave orders for his execution in the Tower without Edward's knowledge.

Unfortunately, Edward IV, who had been fooled by Richard's show of loyalty, died unexpectedly, probably as a result of his dissolute life, but not before naming Richard as protector of the realm and protector of his young son, Edward, the heir to the throne.

After King Edward's death, Richard, advised by Hastings, moved quickly to seize the throne. Feigning loyalty to the young King Edward V, he swore a public oath of allegiance at York, but moved to intercept his party at Northampton which was travelling from Ludlow to London for the coronation. Perhaps aware of the threat posed by Richard, Earl

Rivers failed to meet Richard as agreed at Northampton but progressed to Stony Stratford. Rivers met Richard for supper, and the following morning the duplicitous Richard arrested him and rode to Stony Stratford where he surprised the King's party, arrested Richard Grey and Thomas Vaughan, and took charge of Edward. Rivers, Grey and Vaughan were packed off to the North, Richard's stronghold, where they were later executed without due process of justice. Despite his protestations, Edward was compelled to accompany his uncle and was taken under his protection.

Edward Woodville, like others of the Woodville family, having good cause to doubt Richard's good faith, finally sought refuge in Brittany, after securing much of the treasury from Richard's hands. Elizabeth Woodville, the late king's wife, with her eldest son in Richard's power, and fearing for herself and her children, sought sanctuary for both them and herself in Westminster, together with her brother, the Bishop of Salisbury

Richard had Edward secured in the Tower, beyond the help of those who might have sought to render him assistance.

As Hastings had assisted Richard because he wished the young King Edward to be removed from the grip of the Woodvilles in order to curtail their ambition, so, remaining a firm supporter of Edward's succession, he baulked at Richard's ambition and his treatment of the boy, and thus felt obliged to turn against his once close ally.

Knowing that there was opposition to his intention to usurp the throne, Richard split the Council so that it met in two parts, in order to remove those standing in his way. At the meeting in the Tower, soldiers, following a pre-arranged signal, burst into the meeting and arrested Hastings, Stanley, Archbishop Rotherham and Bishop Morton. Although the others were spared, Hastings, Richard's former friend, was taken to Tower Green and summarily executed.

Despite having control of Edward, Richard could not believe his position secure while Richard, the king's younger brother, remained with his mother. Accordingly, when, by use of threats and promises, Elizabeth had been persuaded to surrender this boy to him, he was sent to the Tower to accompany Edward.

With the strength of the opposition to his proposed usurpation becoming evident, he ordered troops from the North to intimidate any who might rally against him.

After his declaration of the illegitimacy of both princes in the Tower, the path was finally cleared for Richard to grasp the crown, much against the will of the people. Yet Richard had not finished with the princes. Their imprisonment, he calculated, failed to provide sufficient security, for while they lived they would always be a focus for discontent and potential rebellion. Thus, he plotted their murder, and they began to be seen less and less frequently, until they disappeared from view completely. However, such a cruel act of murder lay beyond the conscience of the Constable of the Tower, Sir Robert Brackenbury, and Richard was compelled to send James Tyrell to slaughter them and bury them secretly. When rumours of the death of the young boys began to circulate they were met with genuine outpourings of great sorrow for young lives cut short, and with growing revulsion against the tyrant king who could so act against the laws of God and man. The fate of the innocent young princes inflamed to such an extent the indignation of Henry Tudor, whose forces had been augmented by those fleeing the unhappy country, that he determined to invade England to rid the country of so cruel a tyrant. However, Henry, aided by Buckingham, but hampered by ill-luck and ill-favoured weather, had to abandon his first attempt. Richard, increasingly isolated as a result of his misrule, was forced to execute Buckingham, previously one of his firmest supporters.

Although Henry, who intended to indicate how he would bring peace to a country riven by factions, had gained additional support by his proposed marriage to Elizabeth of York, Richard aimed to frustrate this scheme, by also proposing marriage to Elizabeth, who was his niece, and so hardened opinion against him. So abhorrent was such an incestuous proposal that Richard's advisers persuaded him to a humiliating public denial, and he abandoned the scheme.

Previously profligate in his spending, Richard was forced to re-impose another form of the hated benevolences, taxes under another name.

Henry invaded again, this time at Milford Haven, and, progressing through Wales and the Midlands, garnered increasing support. Meanwhile, Richard, having established himself at Nottingham, moved his army to Leicester to counter the threat.

The two armies met near the village of Bosworth and, though Richard fought bravely to the last, so many of his supporters either deserted him or lacked enthusiasm for the fight that he lost the battle. He was slain as he endeavoured to turn the course of the conflict by attempting a last desperate charge towards Henry.

Henry, harbinger and architect of England's bright future, was crowned on the battlefield with a crown found hanging on a bush, the same crown that Richard had worn into battle.

The naked body of the despised king, bespattered with mud, was slung over the back of a horse and carried back to Leicester where it was exposed to public view before being buried with irreverent ceremony in Greyfriars.

So the main indictments run against Richard. But how far do they stand scrutiny? Was Richard a true monster, or the victim of Tudor propaganda? Perhaps equally the championing of Richard as an exemplary king, the unfortunate victim of Tudor lies, and his denigration as wicked ruler, who met his just reward in battle against the saviour of the country, arise from a simplistic narrative drive to present a canvas of heroes and villains. This book is an attempt to discover what we can truly know about this most controversial king.

Richard's Early Life

If our characters are, to a greater or lesser extent, moulded by the influences of our childhoods and adolescence, it easy to comprehend how Richard might have been affected by the turbulent times into which he was born. Born at Fotheringhay Castle on 2 October 1452, he was the eleventh child of Richard the Duke of York. His mother, Cecily Neville, was the daughter of the Earl of Westmorland.

Richard's childhood was overshadowed by the turmoil occasioned by the Wars of the Roses. He must have been aware of the conflict from an early age, since his father was one of the principal protagonists. Some historians have placed both Richard and his brother George at the pillaging of Ludlow in 1459, when he was barely seven years old, relying on *Gregory's Chronicle*, which seems to indicate that their mother was in the town at the time, believing that they are likely to have been in her care.[1]

> *Also that same yere the Duchyes of Yorke com unto Kyng Harry and submyttyd hyr unto hys grace, and she prayde for hyr husbonde that he myght come to hys answere and to be ressayvyd unto hys grace; and the kynge fulle humbely grauntyde hyr grace, and to alle hyrs that wolde come with hyr, and to alle othyr that wolde com yn with yn viij dayes. And after viij days to done the execusyon of the lawe as hit requyryd. And many men, bothe knyghtys and squyers, come whythe Syr Water Deverose, in hyr schyrtys and halters in hyr hondys,*

> *fallynge by-fore the kynge, and alle hadde grace and marcy bothe of lyffe and lym.*
>
> *The mysrewle of the kyngys galentys at Ludlowe, whenn they hadde drokyn i-nowe of wyne that was in tavernys and in othyr placys, they fulle ungoodely smote owte the heddys of the pypys and hoggys hedys of wyne, that men wente wete-schode in wyne, and thenn they robbyd the towne, and bare a-waye beddynge, clothe, and othyr stuffe, and defoulyd many wymmen.*
>
> *The Duchyes of Yorke was take to the Duke Bokyngham and to hys lady, for they two ben susters, and there she was tylle the fylde was done at Northehampton, and she was kept fulle strayte and many a grete rebuke.*

Following this disaster and their father's flight to Ireland, the boys and Cecily were placed under the care of the Duchess of Buckingham, Cecily's sister, where they stayed for some time under unhappy circumstances. In these dark times they would have been aware that Parliament had condemned the leading Yorkists as traitors, declaring their lives and property forfeit. The young Richard by now had begun to experience how instability in the realm resulting from conflict between powerful factions could impose misery on those caught up in its violence, whether direct participants or not.

Miserable though this time might have been, the boys faced a further upheaval when, in the summer of following year, 1460, they were transferred to the residence known as Fastolf's Palace, where the visits of their eldest brother, Edward, Lord of March, suggests that their time here might not have been without some compensations.[2]

> *Right worschipfull Sir and Maister, I recomaund me un to you. Please you to wete, the Monday after oure Lady Day there come hider to my maister ys place, my Maister Bowser, Sir Harry Ratford, John Clay, and the Harbyger of my Lord of Marche, desyryng that my Lady of York myght lye here untylle the comyng of my Lord of York and hir tw sonnys, my Lorde George and my Lorde Richard, and my Lady*

> Margarete hir dawztyr, whiche y graunt hem in youre name to ly here untylle Mychelmas. And she had not ley here ij. dayes but sche had tythyng of the londyng of my Lord at Chestre. The Tewesday next after, my Lord sent for hir that sche shuld come to hym to Harford (Hereford) and theder sche is gone. And sythe y left here bothe the sunys and the dowztyr, and the Lord of Marche comyth every day to se them.

Yet the misfortunes of war were tragedy and further disruption to the lives of the young boys, following the disastrous defeat of the Yorkists at the Battle of Wakefield in which their father died. They would have been familiar with reports of the battle. Margaret, wife of Henry VI, having fled to Scotland and gathered an army, invaded England and reached Sandal Castle where the Duke of York was staying. Since the chroniclers were in general at this time Yorkist in their allegiance, and unwilling to dwell too much on calamitous defeats, there is some uncertainty about exactly what followed, but it seems that the Duke, under the impression that he could defeat the force gathered outside the fortifications, sallied forth, unprepared for the larger army that lay concealed. The Duke was slain in battle, but Edmund, his second son, was captured fleeing the field. Accounts of what then followed exemplify the unreliability of many of the chroniclers of that period; something that we shall return to in later chapters. According to the *Registrum Abbatiae Johannis Whethamstede*, he was executed in a vile parody of Christ's Passion.

> They stood him on a little anthill and placed on his head, as if a crown, a vile garland made of reeds, just as the Jews did to the Lord, and bent the knee to him, saying in jest, 'Hail King, without rule. Hail King, without ancestry, Hail leader and prince, with almost no subjects or possessions.' And having said this and various other shameful and dishonourable things to him, at last they cut off his head.

However, this story is probably an invention, since other writers record

Edmund being killed during the battle.[3] Perhaps there is some truth in the report that the dead bodies of leading Yorkists were beheaded, the heads then being placed in various locations on the walls of York, with Edmund's wearing a paper crown as a mockery. Yet, as we shall discover later, the record as presented by partisan writers is often embellished and twisted to suit the prevailing power. Perhaps the more gruesome details of the fate of their brother and father were kept from the young boys, but they must have been informed of their deaths. The world began to seem a sea of tragedies and uncertainties to children at the mercy of so much misfortune, and Richard began to yearn for a time of safety and security, when, by action, he could begin to control fate itself.

Since the Duke of York's death, those from the north, perceiving military weakness, rode south in a destructive sweep. The *Croyland Chronicle* recorded what happened in stark terms.[4]

> *The duke being thus removed from this world, the northmen, being sensible that the only impediment was now withdrawn, and that there was no one now who would care to resist their inroads, again swept onwards like a whirlwind from the north, and in the impulse of their fury attempted to overrun the whole of England. At this period too, fancying that every thing tended to insure them from freedom of molestation, paupers and beggars flocked forth from those quarters in infinite numbers, just like so many mice rushing forth from their holes, and universally devoted themselves to spoil and rapine without regard of place or person. For besides the vast quantities of property which they collected outside, they also irreverently rushed, in their unbridled and frantic rage into churches and other sanctuaries of God, and most nefariously plundered them of their chalices, books and vestments, and unutterable crime! broke open the pixes [pyxes- - vessels made of precious metal containing the Sacred Host consecrated at Mass, usually, in the English Church, suspended above the High Altar] in which were kept the body of Christ and shook out the sacred elements therefrom. When the priests and the other faithful of Christ*

in any way offered to make resistance, like so many abandoned wretches as they were, they cruelly slaughtered them in the very churches or church yards. Thus did they proceed with impunity, spreading in vast multitudes over a space of thirty miles in breadth, and, covering the whole surface of the earth just like so many locusts, made their way almost to the very walls of London; all the moveables which could possibly collect in every quarter being placed on beasts of burden and carried off. With such avidity for spoil did they press on, that they dug up the precious vessels, which, through fear of them, had been concealed in the earth, and with threats of death compelled the people to produce treasures which they had hidden in remote and obscure spots...In the meantime, at each gate of the monastery, and in the vill adjoining, both at the rivers as well as on dry land watch was continually kept; and all the waters of the streams and weirs that surrounded the vill, by means of which a passage might by any possibility be made, were rendered impassable by stakes and palisades of exceeding strength; so much so, that those within could on no account go forth without leave first given, nor yet could those without in any way effect an entrance. Our causeways also and dykes, along which there is a wide and even road for foot passengers were covered with obstacles, and trees, spread along them and laid across, caused no small impediment to those who approached in an opposite direction. For really we were in straights, when word came to us that this army, so execrable and so abominable, had approached to within six miles of our boundaries. But blessed be God who did not give us for a prey unto their teeth! For after the adjoining counties had been given up to dreadful pillage and spoil, (that we may here confess the praises of God in that in the time of His mercy, He regarded the prayers of the contrite, and in his clemency determined to save us from the yoke of this calamity) our Croyland became as though another little Zoar, in which we might be saved; and, by Divine grace and clemency, it was preserved.

Even allowing for some exaggeration, this must have been a terrifying period for many in England. This England of pillage, violence and sacrilege, this country where even the king was vulnerable and where churches were attacked, this was the land of Richard's childhood.

The shifting fortunes of war continued to dog the boys. Though it seemed for a while that events were moving in favour of the House of York when Edward defeated the Earls of Pembroke and Wiltshire at the Battle of Mortimer's Cross, defeat at the Second Battle of St Albans proved to be a major reverse. It was feared that the Lancastrians would be able to take London. Richard and George, packed off to Utrecht, where it was hoped they would be safe under the protection of the Duke of Burgundy, were, for the time being, out of immediate danger.

Meanwhile, fortune had turned once again. London merchants in the generally Yorkist capital were convinced to swear allegiance to Edward by Charles, Duke of Burgundy, on pain of losing valuable trading rights. Proclaimed king on 4 March 1461, supported by Warwick's army, and backed overwhelmingly by his capital, Edward marched to give battle at Ferrybridge; and then, following victory in this small engagement, he went on to face the Lancastrian forces in the decisive Battle of Towton on Palm Sunday, 29 March. A blizzard raged across the battlefield that day making conditions even worse for the men who fought in what is usually regarded as the bloodiest battle fought on English soil. The fighting was so ferocious, with no quarter to be given by either army, that for the first time in an English battle the front lines were forced to a standstill by the piles of corpses which had to be dragged away. After strenuous resistance, the Lancastrian lines finally buckled and their forces were routed. The bridges collapsed under the weight of their numbers, submerging men in the icy waters below. Since bridges now offered no means of escape from the fury of Yorkists, some struggled desperately to cross the rivers but were drowned in the attempt, while others, trapped on the banks, were cut down. So great were the numbers of dead lying in the water that it was said it was possible to ride across the River Cock, over the bodies of the fallen. Perhaps some battle-wearied warrior did perform this grisly ride; maybe it was simply rhetoric and the dead were spared at least this indignity.

The battle lasted until *"the tenth hour of night"* by which time it has been estimated that there were between 20,000 and 30,000 killed. Such high casualties might have resulted from the orders to give no quarter and from the desire of both sets of commanders to bring an end to the wars that had plagued the land for so long. George Neville, brother of Warwick, promoted to the See of Exeter by the new king, grateful for his family's assistance, wrote that the slaughter continued until *"so many dead bodies were seen as to cover an area six miles long by three broad and about four furlongs"*.

Apparently, Edward's brothers meanwhile were being well-looked after by the Duke of Burgundy, and Prospero Camulio wrote on 18 April 1461.[5]

> *Since I wrote today of the two brothers of King Edward who have arrived, one eleven [this must be an error; Richard was eight years old], the other twelve years of age. The duke who is most kind in everything has been to visit them at their lodging, and showed them great reverence.*

But there was to be no tarrying here for any length of time, congenial as it might be, for they were summoned back to England that same month, to a land their elder brother now ruled. Once back in England, George and Richard were welcomed in London with great ceremony.[6] The guilds agreed to greet *"the Lords George and Richard, brothers of the Lord King, in their liveries according etc. and that the Mayor and Aldermen be in crimson"*. After the previous turmoil, things began to seem very much brighter as the *"sun of York"* seemed to be shining with the radiance of success; the country could look forward a period of settled rule; and the royal children could begin to imagine a future growing up in the warmth of brotherly protection and patronage. Nevertheless, much of the damage caused by the wars was irreparable.

By this time only three sons of eight, Edward, George and Richard had survived, and three daughters. The alternating fortunes of the family, continual changes of residence and intermittent threats to their security which had so affected the boys were perhaps coming to an end; yet the background of strife was an unfortunate, and possibly distorting, influence on their developing personalities.

Edward was crowned on 28 June 1461 and, in preparation for their future positions of power and influence, while at the same time anticipating their importance to the security of the crown, he appointed George Duke of Clarence and Richard Duke of Gloucester. About the same time they were both admitted as knights to the Order of the Bath at the Tower of London. Further honours followed. Clarence became Lieutenant of Ireland, and Richard, still just nine years old, was given the post of Admiral of England. In accordance with their status as brothers to the king, Edward also gave them sufficient land to provide an income to support their new positions. Among the grants that Richard received were the manor of Kingston Lacy, the castle, county and honour of Richmond in Yorkshire, the county, honour and lordship of Pembroke in addition to the position of Constable of Corfe Castle. This grand-sounding title was not quite so impressive at it might seem for his powers were severely limited. He was able to enjoy the profits, but was to have no authority within the counties of the lucrative *"wreck of the sea"*; in addition he was to have *"cognisance"* of death and injury occurring in great ships in the middle of great rivers, but only in the ports of those near the sea. Later, perhaps on 4 February 1462, he was created a Knight of the Garter, the premier order of chivalry, whose home is St George's Chapel, Windsor. This date, however, is disputed; it might have been as late as 1465 or even 1466.

The next few years provided a period of relative stability for the young Richard, who remained under the care of the royal household for four years, possibly living at Greenwich or perhaps in the household of the Archbishop of Canterbury, Bourchier. Then in 1465, as was the custom of the age for high born boys, he and Clarence were sent from the care of their family household to another suitable noble household. They found themselves delivered into the care of the Earl of Warwick for a period of three and half years, where, in the same way as other boys in their position, they completed their education and training. Although this parcelling out of children seems alien to us, it was the accepted method of fitting boys for the lives they were expected to lead as heads of important families. The principal reasoning was, in all probability, that boys were likely to be more obedient and attentive to instructions in households other than their own where familiarity might breed, if not contempt, at least reluctance and indolence. In reality, no doubt, families had as many and varied reasons for adopting the practice as families today who send their offspring to boarding schools.

It is generally thought that while in Warwick's care, the boys spent a great deal of their time at Middleham Castle, one of Warwick's principal residences, though it is not certain. In fact, Warwick also possessed important castles at Penrith, Sheriff Hutton and Barnard Castle, and they may well have spent some in all of these. Agreeing to take the boys into his care was not a completely altruistic act on the part of Warwick, for not only would it cement his relationship with the king and bring him influence through the boys (which influence was to prove of crucial importance later) but he also received a generous payment from the king for his trouble. In 1465 this amounted to £1,000.

Although Richard's movements during this time are difficult to trace, it is possible to place him at Warwick within a year or so and in York for the enthronement of Warwick's brother, George Neville as Archbishop of York. The enthronement and accompanying celebrations were glorious affairs, providing Richard with an insight into the splendour that could accompany power. The planning and organisation of such celebrations was a logistical feat. Just providing and cooking the food was a huge enough task. There were:

Partriges	*500*
Woodcockes	*400*
Curlewes	*100*
Egrittes	*1,000*
Stagges, Buckes, and Roes	*500 and more*
Pasties of Venison colde	*4,000*
Parted dysshes of Gelly	*1,000*

Playne dysshes of Gelly	3,000
Colde Tartes baked	3,000
Colde Custardes baked	3,000
Hot Pasties of Venison	1,500
Hot Custardes	2,000
Pykes and Breames	608
Porposes and Seales	12
Spices, Sugered delicates, and Wafers plenty [7]	

It has often been a matter of speculation whether Richard became acquainted with Anne Neville, whom he would later marry, while he resided with Warwick, and although there is no direct evidence for a meeting, it is reasonable to suppose that they did meet during these celebrations, if not elsewhere. It has further been suggested that their early acquaintance sparked a romance that would later propel Richard towards the marriage despite the difficulties that it would create. This can be merely speculation and ignores the political and financial imperatives that bound the brother of the king. But this is to anticipate.

In 1468 Richard was present at another great event. This time he attended his sister Margaret as she prepared to cross the Channel for her marriage to the Duke of Burgundy to secure the relationship with England, most especially the important trading links. It was from attendance at events such as these that Richard learned the manners and behaviour befitting his station. It was important that great lords learned how to act as great lords, for they were under constant scrutiny. The ability to perform in social settings and create the right impression by following the accepted protocols was essential; the outward show was part of what made a prince or a lord.

However, the year that Richard was sent into the custody of the Earl of Warwick, 1465, was to have a far greater significance for both Edward and Richard as well as for the whole country, for this was the year that Edward informed his council that he had previously secretly married Elizabeth Woodville. According to *Fabyan's Chronicle* the events were as follows.[8]

In suche passe tyme, in moste secrete maner, vpon the firste daye of May, kynge Edward spousyd Elizabeth, late wyfe of Sir Iohn Graye, knyght, whiche before tyme was slayne at Toweton or Yorke Field, which spowsayales were solempnyzed erely in the mornynge at a town named Graston, nere vnto Stonyngstratforde; at whiche mariage was no persones present but the spowse, the spowsesse, the duches of Bedford her moder, the preest, two gentylwomen, and a yong man to helpe the preest sing. After which spowsayals endyd, he went to bedde, and so taried there vpon iii or iv houres and after departed & rode agayne to Stonyngstratforde , and came in maner as though he had ben on hunting, and there went to bedde agayne. And within a daye or ii after, he sent to Graston, to the lorde Ryuers, fader vnto his wife, shewynge to hym that he wolde come & lodge with hym at a certayne season, where he was receyued wit all honoure, and so taryed there by the space of iiii days. In whiche season, she nyghtly to his bedde was brought, in so secret maner, that almooste none but her moder was of counsayll. And so this maryage was a season kept secret after, tyll nedely it muste be discoueryd & disclosed, by meane of other whiche were offeryd vnto the kynge, as the queen of Scottes and other.

Elizabeth Woodville

This astounding and unwelcome news took by surprise even those close to him, who were well aware of his weakness for good-looking women. Elizabeth with her fair hair and blue eyes was certainly regarded as a beauty in her day, and, though few would have been surprised if they had been told that she was Edward's mistress, they were shocked to learn of the king's marriage to a woman so clearly a social inferior, the widow of a Lancastrian knight with two sons by him, the first commoner to marry a king since the coming of the Normans. Of course, in some ways, this marriage appears to foreshadow that disastrous union between Henry VIII and Anne Bolyen, especially since Elizabeth, realising her hold over Edward and unwilling to play the part of mistress, had seemingly insisted on marriage, a marriage that created serious political problems, not as acute as those caused by Henry's marriage, but severe enough to blight not only Edward's reign but the following reign as well. She was said to have heavy-lidded eyes like those of a dragon, a description that, perhaps meant as a compliment to her beauty, hints at the destructive power she was able to wield.

Edward, usually politically adept, was well aware of at least some of the potential political consequences of this match, hence the previous secrecy, but it is unlikely that he calculated the strength and longevity of the waves he had created; yet even if the most serious evils lay in the future, it did not mean that there were no immediate problems. The most important of these was the king's relationship with the powerful Warwick, who had been negotiating a marriage treaty between Edward and Bona of Savoy, a French princess and niece to Louis XI. The news of the Woodville marriage was a serious blow to Warwick's prestige, for he had been placed in a most humiliating position, and made to seem a fool. A further blow for Warwick, who favoured an alliance with the French, was that it destroyed his plans for a treaty with Louis against Burgundy and Queen Margaret. Louis was keen for such an alliance since it was the most obvious way of defeating Burgundy and annexing the dukedom. Edward's disregard for Warwick's labours, political aims and self-respect provided the spark igniting his discontent, which would later become an angry, consuming blaze.

It was, however, the Woodville ambition that was to cause even longer-lasting damage. Elizabeth, lacking the social pedigree of those among whom she was now in frequent contact, aimed to strengthen her position by consolidating and increasing her power. This she achieved by various means. Clearly she had influence over Edward and she made sure that members of the Woodville family gained influence by a series of marriages.

Realising that by levering other members of the Woodville clan into the political world she could buttress her own power with people bound to her by ties of gratitude and family loyalty, she set about marrying her sisters to influential nobles, ignoring the growing disquiet. However, it was not the marriage of the eleven year old Duke of Buckingham to her sister Katherine, a later cause of conflict, that created the most gossip, for, after all, it was not uncommon for princes and nobles to be betrothed at an early age in the wider political interest, it was the marriage of her twenty year old brother, John, to the dowager Duchess of Norfolk, Warwick's aunt, that was branded the *"diabolical marriage"*. She was at least in her sixties, possibly as old as eighty. Warwick was enraged, sensing that this was a blatant bid for power and wealth, which it most certainly was. Anthony, Lord Rivers, another brother, also gained considerable influence and it was he who was to enter the story at a later point, playing a key role in the fate of the young Prince Edward, and in Richard's path to the throne. Additionally, Elizabeth ensured that her supporters were given key positions, further augmenting the numbers of those indebted to her. So successful was she that Mancini reported that she had created a faction in order to *"manage the public and private business of the Crown"*.[9] This faction proved to be a source of discontent and frustration, division and conflict throughout Edward's reign and beyond.

There is almost no documentary evidence about Richard's time in Warwick's household, but we can assume that he would have been given the same education as other boys of his class. The boys of the medieval nobility learned to become fluent in the important languages of the day and were taught to appreciate high culture, including music. Their education also included the highly practical art of horsemanship with the associated skills required for hunting and jousting. It is easy to imagine high-spirited boys enjoying such physical challenges but submitting with an ill-grace to lessons in demeanour and behaviour. The boys had to learn how to behave in the company of others: how to speak and act with the appropriate courtesy, an indication that they were worthy of their rank. They would also have to be familiar with the customary household routines and timings. The main meal of the day was served in the great hall at about eleven o'clock, a formal occasion attended by the whole household. Each man's social status would be reflected in his position at table. Supper was normally at about five o'clock. Boys were expected to observe and learn from these important social occasions so that, when they became lords in their own houses and castles, the appropriate forms and observances would have become second nature. Occasionally, the dark held temporarily at bay by candles, evening entertainments might have been provided, luxuries well-beyond the means of all but the wealthy.

It is not possible to say how far Warwick personally oversaw the education of Richard and Clarence or how frequently they came into contact with him, since he was frequently engaged away from home on the king's business. The subsequent paths taken by the brothers do suggest that their reactions to him were very different.

In 1469 when Richard was sixteen he was brought back to Edward's court, perhaps because his education was now regarded as complete and it was necessary for him to develop an understanding of the role he would have to play as a royal duke and brother to the king, perhaps because Edward now regarded him as mature enough to engage in affairs of state and offer him support, or perhaps because, Edward, growing wary of Warwick's disaffection, sought to remove him from his influence.

The announcement of the marriage revealed the depth of the division between Edward and Warwick over foreign policy. Edward, probably quite aware that the revelation would destroy the negotiations for an alliance with Louis, wished to pursue his alternative policy of forming an alliance with Burgundy. In this Edward was the more practical politician since popular feeling ran far more in favour of Burgundy than France, not least because England had many lucrative trading connections with the dukedom. Moreover, France was regarded as an enemy of long-standing. Warwick, already provoked by the failure of the marriage negotiations and the destruction of his hopes for an alliance with France, was humiliated again when Edward married his sister Margaret to the Duke of Burgundy.

Further evidence of the growing ill-feeling was provided by the refusal of Warwick's brother, George Neville, Archbishop of York, to attend the opening of Edward's parliament, which was met by Edward's retaliation when he removed him from his position as Chancellor.

Warwick, regarding himself as the most powerful magnate in England and smarting from Edward's apparent indifference to the important role he had played in bringing him to power, felt deeply affronted that the Woodvilles, a family of little distinction, yet growing in influence and arrogance, had supplanted him in guiding the affairs of state. Yet there was a further rebuff to his ambition. He had sought to strengthen his political sway with the strategic marriage of his daughter Isabel with Clarence, the king's brother, to his mind an appropriate and obvious union which would establish both families as a formidable combined force. However, Edward, fearing his ambition, wary of the potential danger and perhaps realising that Warwick had more to gain from the marriage than he did, forbade the match. Disparaged and undervalued by a king who ought to have cherished and rewarded him, Warwick calculated that since his support was vital in maintaining Edward's crown, the removal of that support to another candidate would be advantageous. After all, if he was powerful enough to battle Edward's path to the throne, he could as easily pitch him off that princely seat, replacing him with a more grateful king who would welcome his experience and guidance. The obvious candidate was Clarence.

Perhaps Edward's treatment of Warwick and the promotion of the Woodvilles can be regarded as serious miscalculations, a failure to understand both the depth of Warwick's resentment and the necessity of his support, and an over-reliance on a resented and grasping faction. It is easy to make the judgement, since we are familiar with its consequences. Yet, Edward was in a political bind. It is true that the advancement of the Woodvilles created more problems than it solved, but Warwick created a separate problem. Clarence and Richard were not old enough to be given real power and so were unable as yet to provide support. If Warwick became too powerful he would not only become a permanent threat to Edward but might possibly oppose any future move on Edward's part to create a formidable alliance with his two brothers, nobles who could rule huge swathes of the country on behalf of the crown. It is certainly possible that Edward reasoned it was best to try to curtail Warwick's influence as soon as possible. Delay would increase the danger. It was unfortunate for Edward that, in fact, Warwick was already too powerful to be dismissed so lightly. A report to the French king in 1464 had indicated, although in a facetious manner, the precariousness of the political situation in England, since there were two kings in England *"M. de Warwick and another whose name escapes me"*.[10]

It is possible to believe that Clarence, who had supported Warwick in his pursuit of a French alliance, changed his allegiance from Edward to Warwick as a result of Warwick's influence during his adolescence. There is no direct evidence for this, and another explanation is that Clarence, ambitious and disloyal, simply grasped at the opportunity to seize the crown for himself. Warwick and Clarence in calculated disobedience to Edward pursued their plans for Clarence's marriage with his cousin Isabel and, after having received permission from the Pope, the two were married on 11 July 1469 in Calais, which location had the twin advantages of being under Warwick's governorship and far enough from the reach of Edward.

Even if the serially unreliable Clarence had been swayed by his youthful association with Warwick, Richard did not follow his lead, remaining determinedly loyal to Edward. This emphasis on loyalty would become a marked feature of Richard's character. He even adopted the motto *Loyaltie me lie (Loyalty binds me)*, perhaps as one way of trying to impose some permanence, even if only at a personal level, on a world whose instability had so disrupted his childhood and whose changes and chances were ever-likely to bring misfortune and calamity. A rebellion under the apparent leadership of Robin of Redesdale, but almost certainly inspired by Warwick, demanded the removal of the grasping Woodvilles and Herberts from the positions they had usurped from the rightful lords. Warwick had the further aim of removing Edward and replacing him with Clarence, probably under the pretext that Clarence was the rightful king, since Edward was barred by reason of illegitimacy.

The claim that Edward was illegitimate has been the subject of much debate. There are three main strands of evidence. Dr Michael K Jones's research has revealed that at the likely time of conception Richard, Duke of York, was away on campaign, from 14 July to 21 August, 1441, several days' march from Rouen where Cecily was residing, but there is, of course, the possibility that Cecily paid him a visit during this time, or that the birth was premature, though a birth that early was unlikely. The baptismal ceremonies provided for Edward and his younger brother Edmund provide an interesting contrast. Edmund's was a grand, public occasion, celebrated in the main part of the cathedral, whereas Edward's was conducted in private in a side chapel with very little fuss, as though to avoid drawing attention to the child. Strange as this might be, it is insufficient to support the claim of illegitimacy. Mancini, who was spying on behalf of the Archbishop of Vienne, wrote in his report that when news of Edward's marriage to Elizabeth reached Cecily, so enraged was she that in her fury she declared Edward to have been conceived in adultery and was prepared to make this testimony in public. This appears to be the most compelling of the three pieces of evidence, though it has been suggested that this was merely an outburst of rage at the knowledge of Edward's marriage to the commoner Elizabeth Woodville. However, there are problems with Mancini's reliability. As he spoke no English he must have been reliant on interpreters and other people's accounts; his main source appears to be have been Dr John Argentine who was no friend to the

Yorkists; he makes a number of important errors in his report; and, since he arrived in England at the earliest at the end of 1482, and possibly not until March/April 1483, returning to France shortly after Richard's coronation, which took place in July 1483, he had no first-hand knowledge of most of the events he describes.

To put down the uprising, Edward rode north through East Anglia where it is recorded that Richard recruited four men under his own banner. However, realising that the rebels had raised a greater army than he had anticipated, Edward sought the protection of Nottingham Castle

With Robin of Redesdale, building on the discontent engendered by high taxes, the debasing of the coinage and hatred of the Woodvilles, achieving success in the north, the time was advantageous for Warwick and Clarence to march north with their powerful army to take advantage of the defeat that the rebels had inflicted on Edward's army at the Battle of Edgecote Moor. Warwick showed little mercy to those who fought for the king in the days following. The Duke of Devon, the Duke of Pembroke and his son and were pursued, caught and executed. The queen's father, Earl Rivers and John, her brother, the husband in the *"diabolical marriage"*, were captured, and Warwick, overcome with the desire for vengeance and resentment at the supposed insult that John's marriage to his aunt had caused, laying aside any delicate political considerations, had these men executed, too. The greatest prize, however, was King Edward, who was discovered near Kenilworth, taken prisoner and delivered into the custody of George Neville, Archbishop of York. If the loyal Richard had accompanied Edward in his campaign against the rebels, as has been supposed, he escaped capture.

Made over-confident by his success, Warwick had acted impetuously in executing the queen's father and brother, but then he saw no reason for restraint. He had proved himself powerful enough to overcome the king and his supporters. This was but another in a series of rash acts that drummed men to the battlefield and so prolonged the Wars of Roses. On the other hand, he declined to execute the king, which was possibly another error, considering the path of rebellion that he had elected to follow. Perhaps his over-confidence led him to believe that even alive Edward would be unable to pose a credible threat; perhaps he hoped that by forcing Edward to abdicate, Clarence could take his place in an ordered and superficially legitimate succession. Certainly he wished to destroy the Woodville influence and perhaps a suitably chastened and compliant King Edward, even more reliant on his power, would restore his political fortunes. In pursuit of his desire to release the Woodville grip on the king, he sought to persuade him that Elizabeth, trained in the black arts by her mother, had practised witchcraft on him. It is hard to say how credible such an accusation sounded, but it certainly provided an explanation, for what was otherwise, in the eyes of most people, hard to accept, the rise of the Woodvilles.

The capture of the king, a significant success for Warwick, proved to be the cause of his failure. He had over-estimated the strength of his position and the loyalty of his support. The Woodvilles might have been generally disliked, but with the deposed Henry VI still incarcerated there was little enthusiasm for the uncertainty caused by the imprisonment of another king. Opposition, therefore, rallied against Warwick who, suffering from the inability to raise sufficient forces, found support lacking even from his brother, the Earl of Northumberland. Edward's policy of allying himself with Burgundy paid off; the Duke, married to Edward's sister threatened an invasion. Edward was removed to Pontefract. Meanwhile, it is likely that Richard, motivated by the plight of his brother, stepped up his recruitment, and when he and Hastings arrived at the head of a large army they secured the release of the king. Edward was received with much rejoicing and jubilation when he returned to his capital, indicating that he still retained his former popular appeal.

Yet, the situation was delicate. Edward, maybe reasoning that since it was doubtful he had the power to punish the rebels and that his authority would be better secured by showing mercy, issued a general pardon. Clarence was accepted back and even Warwick escaped any serious consequences, merely forfeiting some of his land and titles.

There was an appearance of contrition and absolution. The appearance, however, belied the underlying reality. For the brothers, the rebellion had been a defining period in their relationship with the king. Both had been under Warwick's influence, but only one had been so disloyal as to join him. Presumably, Richard had also come under pressure at some point either from Warwick or from Clarence, or from both to desert his brother, but he had maintained his allegiance. Clarence, whose impetuousness and waywardness might otherwise have been overlooked by Edward, had taken the path from which there could be no recovery of genuine trust, no matter what face both of them might put on matters. Edward might hope that Clarence could change and become a stalwart supporter, but in reality he knew that he would never be able to forget the disloyalty of his brother and that truly Clarence was too volatile to be trusted. For his part Clarence, too, must have realised the truth of the matter. Richard's loyalty in Edward's time of need would always cast a darker cloud over his own betrayal. Whether or not Edward should or could have dealt more decisively with Warwick, there was little chance that he would truly submit to Edward's rule for in the words of the *Croyland Chronicle* his was *"a mind too conscious of a daring deed"*. Edward might hope that Warwick would once again prove to be a bulwark of royal power, but Warwick was a character far more likely to fret over missed chances and to seek ways of recovering what had been lost than to bow to misfortune.

Richard received his rewards, which included substantial estates. He was appointed constable for England and, Edward, realising how useful and effective he was, later in the year gave him effective control of much of Wales by appointing him chief justice for the north of Wales, chief steward, approver and surveyor of the principality of Wales and the earldom of March in England, Wales and the Marches. Richard could be trusted to act as the king's viceroy to keep control of the further edges of his kingdom. A rebellion in Wales in 1469 gave Richard, who was just seventeen, the chance to prove his ability by putting down the uprising and by reducing and subduing the castles of Carmarthen and Cardigan. Edward's faith in him was justified and Richard received his reward in 1470. He was made king's steward in the south of Wales, chief justice of south of Wales (which complemented his position in the north) and was granted the stewardship of other lands. However, Richard's merited gains might also have been designed to thwart Warwick who wanted to establish his influence in the principality. Furthermore, when Richard was appointed to the Duchy of Lancaster, Warwick received a further snub and curtailment of his power, for Richard took the place of Lord Stanley, his brother-in-law.

Warwick also had to contend with the animosity of the Woodvilles who wanted revenge for the execution of the queen's father and brother. This determined opposition of those who comprised the most influential group prevented him from clambering back to the summit of power and, moreover constituted a continuing menace. The balance of power between Warwick and the Woodvilles was, therefore, unstable and, given Warwick's character and grievances, was never likely to remain long without strife.

A rising in Lincolnshire, led by Lord Welles and Dymock, had been suppressed when pardons were offered, though the son, Sir Robert Welles, continued his opposition by declaring for Clarence and Warwick. Edward achieved an early victory at Lose-Coat Field and captured Sir Robert. Meanwhile, Warwick and Clarence were leading an army from the Midlands with the professed aim of aiding the king. However, Sir Robert's confession provided evidence that Edward was wise, or at least lucky, in his decision to make an early end of the rising, since the intention of Warwick and Clarence may well have been to lend their support to the rebels. What makes this even more likely is that Warwick had used the same tactics with the Robin of Redesdale rising: encourage a supporter to initiate a rebellion sufficiently large to require the king to engage his forces to suppress it, enter the conflict later at an opportune time and hope to emerge victorious. Richard took no part in this conflict, apparently busy with affairs in Wales, though Kendall has suggested that an argument between Richard and Stanley's followers resulted in Richard informing Edward of Stanley's disloyalty, the communication of which persuaded Stanley, the notorious opportunist, to abandon the plans he had of joining Warwick.[11]

Warwick and Clarence, aware of the danger, decided on flight and, making their way to the West Country to sail for France, avoided Richard who, possibly too late, had been commissioned to recruit men from Devon and Cornwall, following a similar commission for Herefordshire and Gloucestershire.

His previous pro-French stance ensured that Warwick, now seriously weakened following the vacillation of the self-interested Stanley and the failure of his brother the Earl of Northumberland to lend him support, found a friend in Louis. Louis, however, had his own reasons for being particularly welcoming, since Warwick, although at present stripped of most of his power and in exile, provided the best prospect of bringing about an Anglo-French alliance against Burgundy. For Louis, providing a refuge was a chance worth taking as, Edward's kingship being in the balance, Warwick might yet prove to be a power in the land again - Kingmaker once more.

Indeed, Warwick did begin to scheme a return. Queen Margaret, wife of the deposed Henry VI was also living in France. Although both were suffering exile, it seemed most unlikely that they would ever be reconciled. Margaret bore an understandable hatred and resentment towards Warwick for his part in placing Edward on the throne in Henry's place, and her feelings ran so high against him that she was reported as saying *"with the honour of her and her son, he and she might not, nor could not pardon the said Earl, which hath been the greatest causes of the fall of Henry"*.[12] Margaret perhaps felt constrained to at least make a pretence of thoroughly loathing Warwick, for any other reaction might seem to cast some doubt on the depth of her support for her husband; or perhaps political reality and ambition could provide a sufficient reason for suppressing personal emotions. Whatever her true feelings, she was persuaded to a reconciliation with Warwick. The agreement was made that when Henry was restored to his throne, Warwick's daughter, Anne, would marry Margaret's son, the Prince of Wales. Even if an alliance with Warwick was disagreeable in the extreme, it had the advantage of providing a way of settling the score with the House of York, a far more detestable enemy, and of regaining power. For Warwick, too, with the additional promise of aid from Louis, it offered a realistic prospect of re-establishing himself at the centre of power. Those who played for high political stakes had to be prepared, if necessary, to sacrifice personal feeling as a price for entry to the game. However, it was not always the key players themselves who paid the price of their scheming and manoeuvring, as Clarence must have realised. His support for Warwick was not equally reciprocated once Warwick calculated that it was worth abandoning Clarence's bid for the throne in favour of restoring Henry and re-establishing the House of Lancaster.

Meanwhile in England, Edward, fully aware of the importance of the powerful northern lords, and understanding that with Warwick a declared enemy, rather than an ally, he was vulnerable, removed Warwick's brother from his earldom in Northumberland, replacing him with Henry Percy; he also restored Barnard Castle to Bishop Booth, who seems at this time to have earned the trust of the Yorkists.

Despite his attempts to secure his position, Edward was unable to prevent the inevitable. The crushing defeat at Towton notwithstanding, the Lancastrians, still able to muster some forces, and, unwilling to let the opportunity to remove Edward slip by, bolstered the invasion led by Warwick and Clarence, who crossed the Channel in ships paid for by Louis. The most important and unexpected defector to Warwick's cause was John Neville, who, still smarting after being removed from his dukedom, anticipated that he would be better rewarded if Henry were to be restored to the throne.

Thus, Edward was too weak to resist the invasion and, realising that he now had too few forces to give battle, followed the most prudent course by fleeing the country with a small number of his most loyal followers, who had good reason to wish to escape the clutches of Warwick. They were fortunate to evade capture by John Neville, but were forced into a humiliating departure from Kings Lynn in three small boats. Luck again came to their assistance when they avoided a larger force of eight pirate ships, though they were forced to land near Alkmaur on the Friesland coast. The haste of their departure had been so great that, lacking any other means of rewarding the captain of his ship, Edward presented him with his robe lined with sables, and accompanied it with a promise of greater reward in happier future times. Since the Duke of Burgundy was wary of the new regime in England and feared that any provocation on his part might renew plans for the Anglo-French alliance, Edward and his small party were received instead at The Hague.

The victorious and supremely confident Warwick entered London in triumph on 6 October 1470, and released Henry VI, who made a pathetic spectacle, from his long imprisonment in the Tower. His clothes were so shabby and demeaning to a king that he had to be given a blue robe to allow him some semblance of dignity. Although he was ceremoniously paraded through the streets and although he was brought to St Paul's in great pomp to celebrate his restoration, all knew that he was but the shadow king, Warwick being the prime mover. None were more aware of the true disposition of power than those attending parliament, who were intimidated by Warwick's army stationed in the precincts. Warwick created Clarence Lord Lieutenant of Ireland and gave him estates owned by the House of York. He had to be satisfied with what Warwick had deemed appropriate to give him. In effect he had formally surrendered any claim to the throne; he would only become king should the line of succession, now formally settled on Edward, Henry's son, and his heirs, fail.

Richard, whose loyalty was tried again, decided to follow Edward into exile, a course dictated by the store Richard placed on loyalty. If fine sentiments are but words on golden bubbles until tested, this was a true trial of Richard's words. That is not to claim Richard might not also have taken practical considerations into account. Although his time in Warwick's household had him given a claim to friendship and although Warwick possessed the power to make and break kings and there were obvious attractions in supporting this powerful lord, the Kingmaker, there was yet a question of how securely he could remain in favour if his past loyalties and claim to the throne proved to be a storm waiting to break over the Lancastrian dynasty. Richard reckoned that the loyalty providing him with an anchor of conscience in this age of moral and political chaos would also be his best safeguard .

Elizabeth, Edward's wife, who had taken up residence in the Tower in the interests of safety, on hearing the news of Warwick's entry into London, escaped in a barge with her three daughters to sanctuary at Westminster. Here the much-longed-for son was born on 1 November 1470. He was named Edward and baptised with a scant ceremony which was all that that grim place could afford. This child, born in effective captivity with a father in exile, would have been, but a short time earlier, hailed as a prince of the realm and have been greeted with delight by a king overjoyed by the sight of his heir. But then mischance was to tether itself to the short life of the unhappy boy. Ironically, this boy, his name often neglected, and remembered usually as merely one of the "Princes in the Tower", would become the subject of one of the most enduring mysteries of English history and the centre of a loud and continuing controversy.

However, his birth created an additional problem for the Lancastrians since Edward IV now had an heir, who, although residing in England, was out of reach in sanctuary. They could have decided to breach sanctuary by the open use of force, but, as Edward was still alive, the political cost of such an outrage outweighed the potential gain in removing the child. The small party, therefore, survived, but only with assistance of loyal friends, who provided them with food and supported them.

Warwick, now with a firm grasp on power, wasted little time in pursuing his long-held aim of a French alliance - thus reversing the previous policy of Edward – and in February 1471 England declared war on Burgundy.

It is recorded, though how accurately it is hard to tell, that when Henry Tudor was presented to Warwick by Jasper Tudor, Warwick was so impressed with the character and intelligence of the boy that he predicted he would one day rule in England.

Initially, Queen Margaret, still exiled in France, seemed reluctant to risk returning to England with her son, Edward of Lancaster, perhaps because she feared the consequences of Warwick's hostility towards Burgundy. However, in characteristic manner, once she decided to return in in the early part of 1471 she refused to concede to the storms that threatened destruction and she eventually arrived on the English shore in April with Edward.

However, it was Warwick's stubborn approach to foreign policy that helped nudge the Fortune's wheel once more in favour of Edward of York. The Duke of Burgundy, whose fears of facing England and France united against him had been realised, saw that there was no longer any reason for holding Edward at a distance. There was no need to placate Warwick and much to gain if he gave support to the Yorkist claimant, should he be successful once again.

Clarence, whose treatment by Warwick rankled, turned his allegiance once again and gladly received the overtures made by the Yorkists. It is possible that for once he understood where his loyalties should lie and that he made an informed choice, but it is far more likely that headstrong and unreliable, fretting at Warwick's apparent ingratitude, he simply bounced back to his brother, hoping for more favourable treatment. Richard and Clarence exhibited sharply contrasting traits of character: Richard, steadfast, loyal, determined; Clarence, vacillating, untrustworthy and unable see any serious endeavour through to its conclusion.

Edward IV

Edward's exile did not last long, for in March 1471, assisted by the Duke of Burgundy and carried across the Channel in ships of the Hanseatic League, he made an unsuccessful attempted to land in Norfolk. Here his small force of about 2,000 was unable to overcome forces probably led by the Earl of Oxford's brother and so he sailed up the coast to Ravenspur near Hull. Here both he and Richard landed and marched to York. Because his forces were small he could ill-afford to lose men in unnecessary conflict, and so in order to appease those who would have opposed any attempt of his to regain the throne he claimed that he sought only to be restored to his title of Duke of York and would do nothing to disturb the peace of the kingdom. By this subterfuge he was allowed to enter the city unopposed. However, after his threat to execute the city's recorder, if he were pressed to make a formal oath in York Minster, his true intentions began to become clear. As Edward progressed towards Coventry gathering enthusiastic support, Warwick gathered an army at Leicester to prevent his insurrection. Clarence, now persuaded to a reconciliation with his brother, was received, kneeling in submission. His was a critical defection from the Warwick cause and no matter what doubts Edward might have entertained about his sincerity, he could ill-afford to spurn his support and the 4,000 men he brought with him. Edward rejected making a direct attack on Warwick, who by now was secure in his stronghold at Coventry, and opted for the more favourable opportunity offered by an attack on London, which was being held by George Neville, Archbishop of York. Henry, always at the mercy of those who sought to manipulate him, was paraded through the streets in a pathetic and futile attempt to rally support against Edward's approaching army. Fabian recorded the event.[13]

> *And for to cause the citizens to bear their more favour unto King Henry, the said King Henry was conveyed from the palace of Paul's through Cheap and Cornhill, and so about to his said lodging again by Candlewick Street and Watling Street, being accompanied with the Archbishop of York which held him all that way by the hand...the which was more like a play than the showing of a prince to win men's*

hearts, for by this means he lost many and won none or right few, and ever was showed in a long blue gown of velvet as though he had no moo to change with. [Possibly the same blue gown as he had been given on his release from the Tower.]

This desperate show did nothing to persuade the people that Henry, whom everybody knew was incapable of ruling, was a figure worthy of their support. For the Londoners who were, overwhelming Yorkist in sympathy, it was not as though by refusing to rally to the support of the feeble Henry they were guilty of disloyalty to their king, for they had their own king, Edward, and, in any event, they recognised in Henry nothing more than a confused puppet.

Henry VI

Edward entered London to the great delight of the city, which welcomed him back as its king and a man worthy of that great office.

London was a significant strategic prize and the key to Edward's successful campaign. Warwick hastened south to give battle, unwisely refusing to wait for the expected reinforcements that would soon arrive with Margaret. In the event, Margaret would land at Weymouth on the day of the battle itself, too late to offer any assistance or to provide a distraction for Edward's forces.

Edward, expecting Warwick's approach, sent out scouts, who discovered his army of about 15,000 somewhere outside the village of Barnet. Accordingly, Edward drew up his forces, numbering about 11,000, in battle lines at night close to the village, with Richard commanding the right flank. However, in the dark, he probably positioned his army closer to Warwick than he intended, which was an appropriate beginning for a battle in which misunderstanding and confusion spread across both sides. The strict silence he imposed on his waiting troops proved to be well-judged, for Warwick, hindered by the fog of the morning and believing Edward's army to be lying further off, launched an artillery bombardment which largely passed over their heads. The confusion continued as the main battle commenced, with Richard's right wing overwhelming Warwick's left flank while Edward's left flank gave way under pressure from Warwick's right. The fighting then began to be concentrated in the middle. In further confusion, the Lancastrians who had tried to regroup were mistakenly identified as Yorkists and were attacked by their own forces. It is possible that the similarities of the Earl of Oxford's device (a star with rays) to Edward's (a sun in splendour), combined with the poor visibility contributed to the error. Amid cries of "Treason!" the Lancastrians became disheartened and fled. Warwick was slain and his brother, John, was killed by one of his side as he tried to dress himself in Edward's livery. Both bodies were taken to St Paul's and, stripped of their clothing, were placed on public display, so that all could witness that they were truly dead and could no longer offer any opposition to the restored king. In this, the first true battle where he had been tested as a commander, Richard, despite receiving a wound, acquitted himself admirably.

Characteristically, Margaret, while in refuge at Beaulieu Abbey, although initially labouring in despair at the lost opportunity and disheartened by the fate of Warwick, eventually, prompted by the stalwart support of her allies, rediscovered her determination; and with a return of her indomitable courage, refused to consider the defeat at Barnet as the end of Lancastrian hopes. She made an advance through the West Country and when the city of Gloucester closed its gates against her, she discounted being drawn into an assault which would leave her forces vulnerable to a rearward attack by Edward's advancing army, and turned instead towards Tewkesbury.

The Duke of Somerset, leading Margaret's army, might well have hoped to shun a battle at this point, being insufficiently prepared, but because of the fear of being trapped while crossing the River Severn in attempt to seek safety in Wales, he had to face Edward's army.

On Saturday 4 May 1461, Richard commanded the first wave of attack against Somerset's army just outside Tewkesbury. The difficult terrain was unfamiliar to him, while Somerset, who had had more time to make reconnaissance of the area was able to counter his advance. However, when Somerset's rear was attacked by 200 spearmen whom he had initially failed to see, he tried to retreat; but with the line of retreat blocked by the River Avon his army was trapped and cut down on what became known as the Bloody Meadow. Edward then launched a successful attack on the forces led by the eighteen year old Edward, Prince of Wales. When the Lancastrian lines broke, what remained of the fleeing army, desperate for their lives, sought sanctuary in Tewkesbury Abbey. In the rout, the prince himself was killed by men under Clarence's command.

In war, when stakes are high and passions inflamed, it happens that customary courtesies and legalities are neglected, and so it was that the Lancastrian commanders were hauled out of the abbey on the, probably spurious, grounds that the abbey provided no true sanctuary. They were tried in a court over which Richard presided, found guilty of treason, as was the foregone conclusion, and executed.

Polydore Vergil tried to blacken Richard's name by making him complicit in the cruel treatment meted out by the Yorkists.[14]

> *Ther wer taken, Margaret the queen, Edward the prince, Edmund duke of Soomerset, John lord of Saint Johns and xxte moe knightes. All those, except queen Margaret and the prince, wer within two days after deheadyd in the same towne. Edward the prince and excellent yowth, being browght a little after to the speache of king Edward, and demaundyd how he durst be so bowld as to enter and make warre in his realme, made awnswer, with bold mynde, that he came to recover his awncyent inheritance; here-unto king Edward gave no awnswer, onely thrusting the young man from him with his hand, whom forthwith, those that wer present wer George duke of Clarence, Richard duke of Glocester, and William lord Hastinges, crewelly murderyd...*

In the case of Vergil's account of the death of Edward, Prince of Wales, there is sufficient evidence that he is mistaken. A more critical view would be that the distortion of the truth evident here is part of a systematic Tudor vilification of Richard in order to present Henry as the man who saved England from tyranny. According to earlier sources Edward could not have suffered in the manner Vergil describes since he died on the battlefield.

> *And there was slain in the field Prince Edward, which cried for succour to his brother-in-law the Duke of Clarence.*[15]

> *In the wynnynge of the fielde such as abode hand-stroks were slayne incontinent; Edward, called Prince, was taken, fleinge to the towne wards, and slayne in the fielde.*[16]

> *Here is it to be remembred, that, from the tyme of Tewkesbery fielde, where Edward, called Prince, was slayne...*[17]

> *When King Edward IV arrived with his army, he slew Prince Edward in the field...*[18]

> *And in may landid Quene Margaret and prynce Edward her son; and at Tewkysbury met with theym kyng Edward, where was slayne the said prynce Edward...*[19]

Both the responsibility of two battle commands and the duty of conducting the trial placed upon the shoulders of Richard, at a mere eighteen years of age, present a picture of level-headed and able youth whose years of adversity had equipped him with a maturity and self-assuredness that repaid Edward's trust in him.

Margaret, captured following the battle, was taken to London by Edward and confined within the Tower. The day of Edward's triumphant entry into the city was a correspondingly tragic one for the unworldly Henry who, perhaps pleased to end his misery in this life and to join the saints among whom his devotees sought to enroll him as one of their number, died in the Tower. It is impossible to say whether, as the writer of *The Historie of the Arrivall of Edward IV* believed, he died of natural causes on hearing how matters stood, or whether he was hastened to his grave on Edward's orders.[20]

> *The certaintie of all whiche came to the knowledge of the sayd Henry, late called Kyng, being in the Tower of London; not havynge, afore that, knowledge of the saide matars, he toke it so great dispite, ire, indingnation, that, of pure displeasure, and melencoly, he dyed the xxiij. day of the monithe of May. Whom the Kynge dyd to be browght to the friers prechars at London, and there, his funerall service donne, to be caried, by watar, to an Abbey upon Thamys syd, xvj myles from London, called Chartsey, and there honorably enteryd.*

At the very least it seems to be an improbable coincidence that Henry, on the very day when he fell into the power of Edward, who had been ousted from his throne once before, would so conveniently die, and thus no longer remain a figure-head around whom the discontented Lancastrians could rally. It seems likely, therefore, that he was executed by Richard at Edward's command, as is implied by the *Warkworth*

Chronicle.[21]

> And the same nyghte that Kynge Edwarde came to Londone, Kynge Herry, beynge inwarde in presone in the Toure of Londone, was putt to dethe, the xxj. day of Maij, on a tywesday nyght, betwyx xj. and xij. of the cloke, beynge thenne at the Toure the Duke of Gloucetre, brothere to King Edwarde, and many other; and on the morwe he was chestyde and brought to Paulys, and his face was opyne that every manne myghte see hyme; and in hys lyingehe bledde one the pament ther; and afterward at the Blake Fryres was broughte, and ther he blede new and fresche; and from thens he was caryed to Chyrchesey [Chertsey] abbey in a bote, and buryed there in oure Lady chapelle.

What is more unlikely is that a king, who retained at least a huge symbolic importance despite his weakness, was murdered by Richard or at his behest, against the wishes of his brother or without his authority, since Edward was present in the city, and the public display of Henry's body could hardly be expected to pass his notice. On a matter of such grave importance it is barely credible that the young and loyal Richard would act without his brother's warrant. However, that did not prevent those who sought to discredit him from laying such a deed to his charge. Fabian in a guarded description that does not directly accuse him relates that this was the rumour.[22]

> Of the deth of this prince (Henry VI) dyuerse tales were tolde: but the moost common fame wente, that he was stykked with a dagger, by the handes of Glouceter…

And Thomas More, equally unable to blame Richard directly, as so often in his *History*, suggests his guilt by the slippery use of *"as menne constantly say"*.[23]

> He slewe with his owne handes king Henry the sixt, being prisoner in the Tower as menne constantly say, and that without

> *commaundement or knowledge of the king, whiche woulde vndoubtedly, yf he has entended that thinge, haue appointed that boocherly [butcherly] office, to some other then his owne borne brother.*

More supports the assertion that Richard must have committed the deed without Edward's cognisance as Edward, if he had intended the deed, would have entrusted it someone other than his own brother. All of this neatly avoids the problem of lack of any evidence at all, except what is reported as common rumour and gossip; and we are supposed to take both Fabian's and More's word for that.

While Henry's son and heir lived, there was nothing to be gained from seeking his death, since it would transfer the Lancastrian allegiance and bid for power into the hands of his far more capable son; but the death of the prince doomed him, for with his death ended any clear Lancastrian claim. Henry might have lacked the qualities that made a successful king; he might have been a more tool in the hands of more capable and cynical manipulators, but even as the shadow king he could have provided the last obvious focus for Lancastrian discontent.

It was unfortunate for Henry, more saintly than worldly, so unsuited to rule and so thoroughly ill-equipped to navigate the turbulent political waters of the time, that he became the channel through which the ruthless directed the energy of their ambitions. Margaret had hoped to rule through him and, because of the weakness of his reign, the political chaos that ensued had made him the focus for the plots of men such as Warwick. While he lived, the stability of the realm would forever be in question. Edward hoped to establish himself as a strong ruler of a kingdom no longer riven by the Wars of the Roses. With Margaret imprisoned, though later to be ransomed by Louis, and no longer able to command any meaningful support, it would have seemed that finally the Wars of the Roses had come to an end with the House of York victorious. But that was to ignore, or at least to underestimate, the underlying problems caused by the internal factions within the house, the growing resentment between the north and south of the country and the resurgence of the Lancastrian threat, all of which would rack the country with civil war in the following reign. Perhaps Henry, God's fool, entered that heavenly kingdom with more acclaim than he had found on earth and happier than those whom he left behind to contest his throne.

Fauconberg, the illegitimate son of the first Earl of Kent, who had attacked London at the same time as the Battle of Tewkesbury was being fought, had been repelled, and Richard, who had previously proved himself capable of carrying out Edward's wishes successfully, was ordered to capture him. After his surrender to Richard and subsequent escape from Middleham Castle, he was recaptured and executed.

Edward was fortunate, for Richard, having proved his ability and reliability, was of an age to provide a solution to the problem of the north. English kings were reliant on the northern lords to offer a bulwark against the Scots, to provide strong rule in the northern lands and to ensure that the king's writ ran in these far flung edges of his kingdom. Yet it was a political balancing act: to rule effectively the northern lords had to be powerful; but it was a power gathered far from the direct oversight of the king, and such power was potentially dangerous. It was, of course, problems with the Nevilles and the Percys that had been instrumental in rushing Edward into exile. However, with Richard established in the north as a powerful lord, Edward could begin to feel confident that those troublesome lands would be constrained to settle under the sweep of his sceptre and be held tightly within the compass of the royal crown. It was fitting that the stalwart Richard should be rewarded with the lands of the treacherous Warwick. Consequently he was given large grants of land in Yorkshire and what is now Cumbria, in addition to the castles of Sheriff Hutton, Middleham and Penrith, together with associated manors and lordships.[24] Perhaps these castles, which he would have known from his years with Warwick, reminded him of happier days, or maybe symbolised for him the respective rewards and punishment for loyalty and disloyalty. In addition, he was re-granted the titles of Warden of the West March and Keeper of the Royal Forests north of the Trent. He also received the lands forfeited by the defeated Lancastrians and land in the Duchy of Lancaster. However, his estates were not solely northern; he possessed land in Buckinghamshire, Cambridgeshire, Cornwall, Essex, Herefordshire, Hertfordshire, Kent, Lincolnshire, Nottinghamshire and Oxfordshire.

Not only was Richard bound to his brother by ties of loyalty and fraternal affection, but he was dependent on Edward's patronage, unlike those other lords whose titles were more strongly established. For his part, Richard gained not only land and influence, but a measure of security, a stronghold if the storms of change sought to strike him once more. By careful government he consolidated his position, strengthened his place in the hearts of the northerners and inspired firm loyalty in his followers. He hoped to establish himself independent of Edward, not because he wished to challenge him, but because he craved the stability denied him in his younger days, and sensed that the pursuing presence of the grief and misery of that time was always ready to pounce once again. His stout loyalty did not conflict with his need to be independent, strongly founded on his own land and secured by castle walls.

Given their contrasting characters, it was always likely that enmity between Richard and Clarence would break to the surface. However, though their differences had been concealed before, smoothed over by courtly conventions and courtesy, the dispute over Warwick's land in 1471 destroyed any semblance of brotherly unity with an eruption of resentment.

Attainting Warwick with treason was attractive to Edward for political reasons; in addition to which not only would attainder make all his land forfeit to the Crown, but any redistribution of the land would be at his discretion, showing the dependence of any beneficiaries on the king's munificence. Although both Clarence and Richard tried to persuade Edward not to attaint Warwick so that they could be seen to own the land in their own right, they were united in little else. Richard, always wary of what reverses of favour and fortune the future held, hoped to establish a well-founded position, independent of the uncertain favour of others. Clarence having married Warwick's eldest daughter Isabel, saw himself well-placed to make his claim, but was angered by Richard's proposal to marry the youngest daughter, Anne. Some of those inclined to present his human side, in an attempt to counter accusations that Richard was a hard-hearted monster, have proposed that this was a love-match whose beginnings can be traced to the years he spent under Warwick's tutelage when he first fell in love with Anne. This cannot, of course, be ruled out, but it is far more likely that, in common with most marriages between members of this class, it was more strategic than romantic. Richard, who had suffered much on behalf of his brother, saw no reason why he should not share more fully in the spoils of victory. However, Clarence, who hoped to claim Warwick's land by virtue of his marriage to his eldest daughter, exasperated and enraged by what he saw as Richard's calculated attempt at making a claim, hoped to frustrate the marriage. The events that followed take on a melodramatic cast, though, no doubt, to those involved, the drama and perhaps even comedy of the situation was obscured by desperation. Anne disappeared. Not for the first time had Clarence made a crucial miscalculation, for in endeavouring to place her beyond Richard's reach, he had made the prize even more desirable; and Richard, refusing to submit before such a mean-minded plan, hunted for her doggedly, finally discovering her disguised as a kitchen maid in the home of one of Clarence's supporters. Although delighted at his success, he feared that ill-chance had once again attempted to wreck his hopes, and so he forestalled any further interference on Clarence's part by placing her in sanctuary at St Martin-le-Grand. What is less clear is whether the scheming Clarence had forced her into the disguise or whether Anne, with a calm head and a determination of her own, had adopted the disguise in an effort to escape from his clutches. Whatever the truth, Clarence is cast as the dark villain of the piece; and it is easy to credit Richard with a romanticism that he might not have possessed. He has been seen as the gallant knight questing after his childhood sweetheart and releasing her from the grasp of his cruel brother. The truth is more likely to be rather less exciting, less the substance of a cheap romantic novel than the result of hard-headed calculation. For Richard, if he were influenced by the same concerns as others of his time, his interest in Anne's inheritance would have been his principal motivation, especially since control of Warwick's estates in the north would help to confirm him as the pre-eminent lord of the north, in effect King in the North.

What both brothers chose to ignore in their ruthless avarice was the inconvenient truth that the Warwick lands could not descend through the female line, which meant that, no matter what marriages were contracted with Warwick's daughters, his land ought to pass to his next male heir, George, his nephew. The dowager countess held land in her own right, but this would pass to her daughters only on her death. Despite the legal obstacles, Richard and Clarence pressed their grasping claims, as Sir John Paston explained to John Paston in his letter dated 17 February 1472.

> *The king entreats my lord Clarence for my lord Gloucester; and as it is said, he answers that he may well have my lady his sister-in-law, but they shall part no livelihood, as he says. So what will fall I cannot say.*

Anne Neville

The *Croyland Chronicle* gives a good account of the dispute and offers a hint as to why Edward had persevered with Clarence's unpredictability and disloyalty so long: he hoped to win him over finally and bind him to the throne, because the three brothers united would have provided an unbreakable cord.[25]

> *In consequence of this, such violent dissensions arose between the brothers, and so many arguments were, with the greatest acuteness, put forward on either side, in the king's presence, who sat in judgment in the council-chamber, that all present, and the lawyers even, were quite surprised that these princes should find arguments in such abundance by means of which to support their respective causes. In fact, these three brothers, the king and the two dukes, are possessed of such surpassing talents, that, if they had been able to live without dissensions, such a threefold cord could never have been broken without the utmost difficulty. At last, their most loving brother, king Edward, agreed to act as mediator between them; and in order that the discord between princes of such high rank might not cause any hindrance to the carrying out of his royal intentions in relation to the affairs of France, the whole misunderstanding was at last set at rest, upon the following terms ; the marriage of the duke of Gloucester with Anne before-named was to take place, and he was to have such and so much of the earl's lands as should be agreed upon between them through the mediation of arbitrators ; while all the rest were to remain in the possession of the duke of Clarence. The consequence was, that little or nothing was left at the disposal of the real lady and heiress, the countess of Warwick, to whom for the whole of her life the most noble inheritance of the Warwicks and the Despencers properly belonged. However I readily pass over a matter so incurable as this, without attempting to find a cause for it, and so leave these strong-willed men to the impulse of their own wills; thinking it better to set forth the remaining portion of this narrative, so far as it occurs to my memory, with unbiased words, and, so far as I am aware, without any admixture of falsehood therewith.*

Edward, encountering trouble with France, and unwilling either to have his attention distracted or to give Louis any sign of English division and weakness, was exasperated by the antics of his brothers and sought to bring a resolution to their dispute. Initially a compromise was reached. Richard was to surrender his office of chamberlain to Clarence to receive in return *"a part of the grant of castles, honours, lordships, manors and other possessions, late of Richard Earl of Warwick in his right or of Anne his wife"*.[26] Furthermore, Edward agreed to allow Richard's marriage to Anne to proceed. However, in order to distance himself from the antagonism of either brother, Edward sent the matter to a commission which would submit its findings to him for final approval. The final settlement was hardly favourable to the dowager Duchess of Warwick and nephew George. The duchess was to be deprived of her land as though she were dead and George disinherited. The land was to be divided between Richard and Clarence. The outcome, however, hardly satisfied Richard's desire for the stability that an unencumbered title would give him, for Edward, mindful that the required papal dispensation for Richard's marriage might not be forthcoming and, desirous of punishing John Neville's line for his treason by disinheriting them, decreed that Richard would have merely a life interest in the land if there were no male heirs in John's line. As far as Richard was concerned, this was reason enough for continuing to seek a full title. George Neville was among the number of unfortunate youngsters who suffered at this time from the political manoeuvring of their powerful elders. In 1478 he was deprived of his ducal title, on the spurious grounds that he did not have the income to support it, but probably so that he might lose the chance to argue that he was too young to have been in any way involved in his father's treason and influence parliament to reverse the decision to deprive him of his land. Worse for George was that in 1480 he was made a ward of Richard. This gave Richard the opportunity to profit from what lands and income he still possessed, in addition to allowing Richard to arrange his marriage. Although Richard had every incentive to find a wife for George in the hope that he would produce an heir, and thus secure his title to the Warwick lands, George failed to marry and died without issue. Richard, aware that his title to these important estates was not so much carved into their rocks as scratched in the soil, and, fretting about his resulting vulnerability, might later have felt the old insecurities begin to crowd in.

The tantalising lack of information about the dowager Countess of Warwick at this time has given scope for both Richard's defenders and critics to pursue their own lines of argument. The only thing that is clear is that, after she was stripped of her lands, the countess was dependent on Richard, who, already having removed her from sanctuary in Beaulieu Abbey, and taken charge of her, installed her at Middleham Castle with her own servants. The critics, following the unreliable Rous, a priest who chronicled some of the events of the time (about whom more later), maintain that she was imprisoned by Richard and made to pay for the treason of her husband, being kept in miserable circumstances and *"great tribulation"*. However, it is equally possible that, grateful to be released from the confines of sanctuary, under Richard's protection and well-provided for, she lived contentedly enough. A letter discovered at Croft Hall, probably written sometime in 1478, reveals that, even if she were under some form of imprisonment, she was granted at least some freedom of movement for she was to be at *"rob' ho'"* that season. The *"rob' ho'"* mentioned is unexplained, but the implication is that she would be allowed to leave Middleham Castle itself. She survived into the reign of Henry VII.

Following Edward's return to power, his success in defeating and neutralising his enemies diminished the vigour and firmness that former adversity had demanded of him and he began to devote himself to a life of over-eating, licence and excess. With the country seemingly at peace with itself, this lack of attention to political exertion created no great difficulties, and the great lords and land-owners, unwilling to see further dissension and strife, were generally content enough to continue compliantly under this easy-going king.

However, Louis, antagonistic towards Edward as a result of his pro-Burgundian policy, supported the invasion in 1473 led by the Lancastrian Earl of Oxford, who promised a policy more amenable to the interests of France. This earl, who dogged the reign of Edward with his disloyalty and who was to play a key role in Richard's downfall, was a beneficiary of the conciliatory policies of Edward, and had been allowed to inherit the lands of his father, who had been executed for treason; moreover, Edward had created him Knight of the Order of the Bath. Yet these benefits were insufficient to discourage the repeatedly disloyal earl; he had been confined to the Tower in 1468 for plotting with the Lancastrians and, having been released and pardoned, had then joined the successful invasion led by Warwick and Clarence. His men had prevented Edward from landing in Norfolk, but it was his forces, led back from their pillaging to the fight at the Battle of Barnet and wrongly identified as Yorkist, that had caused the fatal confusion in that conflict.

The invasion went badly and, after seizing the stronghold of St Michael's Mount, he was besieged for five months. He submitted only after suffering desertions and receiving a wound to his face. Following his defeat he was imprisoned in Hammes Castle near Calais. Even if Edward were aware, from a list of supporters supplied to Louis, of further treachery on Clarence's part, he preferred to ignore it, not wanting to create a permanent rift with his brother.

Richard, seeking the security afforded by extensive estates, and already in possession of earl's land, sought possession of the earl's mother's land, too, reaching an agreement that, in return for settling her debts and providing an annuity of 500 marks - enough to provide benefices for her son, a Cambridge student -, and other money, she would release the land to him. This agreement has been the focus of further controversy between those who believe that it furnishes an example of Richard's grasping unscrupulousness and avarice, and those who see the open hand of fairness and consideration. The basis for condemning Richard's behaviour is largely to be found in the records of the Court of Chancery, where, after Henry's successful usurpation in 1485, the earl hoped to establish his rights on a firm and indisputable legal footing. The evidence given in the earl's favour relied mainly on the contention that his mother had surrendered the estates only under duress. There was a claim that the countess feared unless she acceded to Richard's demands she would be sent to Richard's castle at Middleham.

She, *"considering her great age, the great journey, and the great cold which then was of frost and snow, thought she could not endure to be conveyed thither without great jeopardy to her life"*[27] The most damning evidence was provided by James Tyrell, who although he had been a supporter of Richard during his reign, had found it convenient to turn his allegiance to Henry. Yet, because his evidence is largely in the form of hearsay and because he was dependent on Henry's favour, it is difficult to believe him to be a reliable witness. The other depositions, based on recollections twenty-three years old, and made by those who had nothing to gain by giving testimony in favour of a dead king - whose vicious reputation was a politically important tool for the Tudors -, and plenty to lose by opposing a powerful Lancastrian earl, who had fought for Henry, are also likely to be unreliable. Morton, a long-time enemy of Richard found in favour of the earl, a decision, the testimonies notwithstanding, that surprised no one, since he was a close adherent of Henry. Yet if Richard had used coercion, it must have been in pursuit of some significant gain. The gain is not immediately apparent, for Richard had been awarded the land by Edward IV for the course of her life, and her sons, attainted with treason, would have been unable to inherit. The countess, gaining some financial security and no longer reliant on the possibly uncertain charity of Edward, might be imagined to have welcomed such an agreement.

If Richard were indeed guilty of an avaricious pursuit of land, this should be understood in the context of his own position. Being the third son he inherited no lands in his own right, lands that could provide him with some insurance against the vicissitudes of English politics. He desired some protection for the ever-changing allegiances of the time and being merely a beneficiary of the king's favour was insufficiently certain. Large, wealthy estates not only provided an important source of income but carried with them concomitant influence and power, which he hoped could insulate him from the sort of turmoil that had so blighted his childhood.

Of course, it was in the north where Richard established himself most securely and where he became the foremost magnate. This was part of Edward's policy of bringing the north under control and of ending the antagonism between the Percys and the Nevilles. However, this created new conflicts, since the politics required careful calculation of the best way to manipulate the aggressive lords and to arrange the blocks of power in the way least likely to cause damage. A key strategy in Richard's approach was to gain the allegiance of the erstwhile Neville supporters. He ensured the allegiance of Sir John Conyers, steward of Middleham, whose influence brought over previous adherents of Warwick, who reckoned that their best fortune lay in allying themselves to this new lord and brother of the king, in the hope that, with previous loyalties put behind them, they might profit in the future. Richard's support was augmented by members of Sir John's extensive family and of the gentry from Cumbria, Durham, and the north and south of Yorkshire.

By assuming Warwick's authority in the north, Richard provoked the enmity of Henry Percy, Earl of Northumberland, a long-standing opponent of the Neville family, who perceived in Richard another contender for pre-eminence. A dispute over Knaresborough provided an excuse to bring resentment to the surface, and proved sufficiently serious as to draw the attention of the king, whose intervention forced an agreement from Richard that he would no longer seek to gain supporters from among the earl's retainers in return for the earl's acceptance of his superior standing. Percy acknowledged this by his agreement to *"do service to the Duke at all times lawful and convenient"*. Richard's possession of Barnard Castle incurred the continuing displeasure of the dispossessed Bishop of Durham, Lawrence Booth. This conflict remained unresolved until Booth was made Archbishop of York in 1476. Stanley remained an obstacle until the reconciliation of 1474.

There were notable advantages to Edward in planting Richard in the north, yet, though Richard owed his position and fealty to his brother, he was no mere lieutenant of the king. Loyal he might have been, but like all capable and powerful people, driven and ambitious, he was not content to become a cypher. As a result, Edward's hopes for a quieter, less fractious north were, at least at first, only partially realised.

Richard's desire for independence, his inclination to tackle difficulties head-on and his warlike disposition threatened war with Scotland and jeopardised Edward's foreign policy. The difficulty arose from their very different concerns: Edward hoped for peace with Scotland which would enable him to invade France, while Richard's reluctance to promote a treaty with the Scots stemmed from his distrust of these troublesome neighbours who continually harassed his northern people. Although prepared to take up arms when necessary, there is no evidence that Richard was a war-mongering warrior, enjoying the clash of arms and battles for their own sake; there was always a purpose to his aggression.

However, Richard and Percy, both recognising that there was little advantage to be gained in prolonged confrontation, and accepting the political reality of the situation in the north, came to an understanding that benefitted not only themselves by removing a distracting conflict but also the people of that part of the land by providing a relatively settled and well-administered government. Percy acquiesced in Richard's position as the most powerful lord in the north, while Richard conceded to Percy control of Knaresborough, the East Riding of Yorkshire and Northumberland. With the spheres of influence agreed, Richard and Percy became allies in organising an effective government for that part of the country. They co-operated in trying to prevent Scottish incursions that had so menaced the north for many years, and in 1477 both received commissions to arrest raiding Scots.[28] Then in 1480 they headed commissions of array *"for defence against certain men of Scotland who have burnt townships and dwellings in the marches and imprisoned and slain the king's lieges"*.[29]

Driven by a desire for military action and by the need to protect their lands Richard and Percy possessed similarities of temperament and purpose, yet there also existed a recognition in both men that to prove themselves capable, interested and just lords, it was often necessary to work in tandem; thus they also strove together to resolve more mundane disputes. In 1476 they ordered in the king's name *"that no man, of whatever condition or degree, make, or cause to be made, any affray or any other attempt, whereby the peace of the king should be broken"*.[30] They were also both commissioned to *"enquire into discords"* that had arisen *"between the king's tenants of the forest of Knaresborough on the one part and the tenants of Lady Berkeley and the abbot and convent of St Mary, Fountains, on the other part, concerning the bounds between the forest and the chase"*.[31]

Whether from a natural instinct to govern well or from a recognition that he needed an enthusiastically loyal following to secure his position, Richard concerned himself with creating a fair and well-ordered administration, and took a personal interest in the operation of justice. This interest was not confined to disputes between the powerful, as might have been expected, but also extended to cases where the interests of the less influential and less wealthy were involved. In a case where a husbandman levied a complaint against the father of one of his supporters, he allied himself to the less powerful party, apparently against his own interest.[32] In the dispute between Richard Clervaux and Roland Place over land boundaries, among other issues, Richard heard the case himself at Middleham Castle and settled the dispute to the satisfaction of both men with a *"friendly suite to be had hensfurth between the sayd parties"*; and in the disagreement between the parishioners of Snaith and the Abbey of Selby over who was to provide religious articles and vestments, he enabled a compromise to be reached.

Justice is but a beggar if it be forced to stand mute outside the doors of the powerful. Recognising this, Richard provided no inequitable protection for those of his household suspected of wrong-doing. When a *prima facie* case was offered against one of his servants accused of abetting a murder, he handed him over to the process of law. Richard was diligent in the administration of justice for it brought solutions to many of the disagreements, grievances and injuries of those under his rule; it could remove the friction and resentments threatening the peace of his lands; and the philosophy of the law matched with its practical application fascinated him.

While the warrior brandishing a battle-sword might inspire and lead his people, the lord holding the sword of justice invites people to his trust and protection. Richard, well-versed in the principles of government, both encouraged support and then inspired loyalty.

An example of the trust that Richard inspired is provided in his appointment as one of the executors for Sir John Pilkington. These executors had a number of duties to discharge including responsibility for the *"wardeshippe and mariege"* of his son. Richard was given the additional responsibility of the care of the boy until the age of sixteen and the administration of his lands until he was married. In an age when avaricious guardians often found the property of their wards a lucrative source of income for themselves, Richard's obligations might be considered to indicate high regard for his probity.

The support of the City of York, a significant economic, religious and intellectual centre, was important for Richard, and so he strove for the affection of its citizens, championing it where he was able. He ordered the destruction of unauthorised garths and weirs which had proved a considerable annoyance and sided with the city over its desire to reduce the fee farm, the sum paid by the city to the crown for its right of self-government.[33] Signalling his desire to be regarded as a committed friend of the city, both he and his wife, Anne, joined the powerful Corpus Christi Guild for the Spring Pageant of 1477. The citizens, aware of the benefits of having such a powerful patron, showed their gratitude by repaying Richard's interest in their affairs. In 1476 he was *"presented with six swans and six pikes"* for preserving their liberties and on 12 March 1482 it was recorded that he had ever *"been a benevolent, good and gracious lord"* to the city.[34]

The goodwill of the people was insufficient in itself to secure Richard's position and so he continued to increase his lands in the north, gaining Scarborough, Helmsley, Cottingham and Skipton even if that meant disposing of land elsewhere.[35] Like Percy, William Dudley, appointed as Bishop of Durham in 1476, having recognised the advantages of working with the king's brother, allowed Richard to extend his influence into the Palatinate of Durham, and brought support for Richard from Ralph Neville of Raby, who presumably saw that his support for Richard might bring advantages and emphasise his loyalty to the king following the execution of Richard Neville, Earl of Warwick.

With Richard establishing control in the north, Edward could afford to turn his attention to France and Burgundy. The obligations imposed by his sister's marriage to the Duke of Burgundy and the importance of England's trading links helped to convince him to support Burgundy in its conflict with France, although this risked creating resentment, since the money to support the war had to be raised by the loathed benevolences, which were in reality unparliamentary taxes. Relying on Richard's political and military experience, Edward placed him in command of about 10% of his forces when they disembarked at Calais in 1475 (ten chevaliers, 100 lances and 1,000 archers). Louis, possibly the more subtle politician, accepting the likelihood of defeat at the hands of the combined English and Burgundian armies, and despairing of divine intervention (*"Ah Holy Mary, even now when I have given thee 1,400 crowns, you do not help me at all"*) responded to Edward's aggressive, if historical, claim to the French throne by offering terms. He agreed to pay 75,000 crowns and a life pension of 50,000 crowns to Edward; sums to other nobles; and offered marriage of the five year old dauphin to Edward's ten year old daughter, together with an annual sum payable to her. Although criticised for weakness, Louis weighed the cost of defeat against coming to terms with Edward and reckoned that in any case he could avoid paying in full once the armies had returned home. For his part, Edward, perhaps influenced by some of his nobles, angered by the inconstant Duke, or frustrated by the Count of St Pol who, instead of allowing Edward to enter the town, had closed his gates against him and fired on his men, considered that it was better to take a golden bribe than to expend a fortune on what ultimately was likely to prove an unwinnable war. Further terms of the treaty created increased opportunities for trade between France and England and allowed a ransom payment of 50,000 crowns for Queen Margaret.

For many on the English side political shrewdness was a poor substitute for military victory and loss of face. Richard, more militarily aggressive and less circumspect than his brother, was so annoyed by what he saw as ignoble capitulation that he distanced himself from the treaty negotiations. Commines, present at the negotiations, impersonating Louis so as to foil assassination attempts heard one knight claim that the disgrace of the Treaty of Piquigny outweighed all Edward's other battle honours. He wrote later that *"The Duke of Gloucester, the King of England's brother, and some other persons of quality, were not present at the interview, as being averse to the treaty"*.[36] It is unclear whether or not Richard was genuinely reconciled to the treaty later. His acceptance of the French king's hospitality and gifts of plate and horses might signal such a change of heart, but equally might mask a spirit placed under subjection by his faithfulness to the principal of loyalty, by political expediency which demanded support for crown, and, on a personal level, by fears that opposition to Edward might leave him exposed.

Louis, forced into a humiliating position, tried to claim a victory. *"I have chased the English out of France more easily than my father ever did; for my father drove them out by force of arms, whereas I have driven them out with venison pies and good wine"*. And yet Louis was not that far wrong, for he had removed the English threat, a threat that was unlikely to return for a while to come at least, since Edward would be unlikely to risk his yearly payments; and as far as Louis was concerned the payments to Edward's daughter would not commence until after the consummation of the marriage. Furthermore, Louis felt he could dishonour the treaty at any time advantageous for himself.

Yet it does not follow that, since Louis gained from the treaty, Edward must have lost, for he had avoided an expensive and prolonged war; Louis had been humbled into paying a type of tribute; he had relieved England from the burden of further taxation; and he had secured the succession to the French throne for a future grandson. Both kings, parading their successes, could legitimately claim to have benefited.

Nevertheless, it is possible to argue that the effects of the treaty were not to be confined to Edward's reign. Even as the medieval period was beginning to transition into the early modern age - a time when the deficiencies of old learning were being exposed by the new, when the traditional structures of society were giving way to a different political reality, when the position of a noble class whose position was reliant on vast landholdings was just starting to come under threat from the new wealth - some parts of the English nobility still retained a vision of their function as the warrior class, a class whose historic function had been to fight. It was not just that they regarded the treaty as a humiliation that was to cause the problem. In waging wars, united in common cause, they found purpose, discipline, and direction for their military energies and ambitions, all of which kept them in obedience to kings willing to channel their aggression. The civil wars had fragmented their loyalties, and with no war to be waged against an external enemy, old enmities and unrest were to break out again under Richard, culminating in the Battle of Bosworth.

However, there was a more immediate difficulty for Edward. Clarence, unstable, disputatious, duplicitous and a continual problem once again showed his disloyalty when the balance of power between France and Burgundy shifted in 1477. After the long years of antagonism between the two rulers, Duke Charles, leading a weakened army was slain at the Battle of Nancy, allowing Louis to lay claim to Artois, Flanders, Picardy and the Duchy of Burgundy itself. Burgundy was vulnerable without an obvious male successor to the dukedom. Although Edward's sister, Margaret, the widow of the Duke, still lived, it was Mary, a daughter by a previous marriage, who had taken control. Aware of the strong links with England, Mary appealed to Edward for help, but Edward now finding himself at the mercy of Louis's previous strategy and realising the double financial burden of providing assistance – which would entail forfeiting Louis's payments and funding a military campaign – he refused.

The problem of Burgundy was not, however, to be dismissed so easily. Margaret, intelligent, politically astute and never a woman to accept thwarted ambition, decided that since Edward was reluctant to provide help, she would seek a suitable marriage to strengthen her step-daughter's position. Although Mary's immense wealth was attractive to many powerful men, Margaret hoped to arrange a marriage with her recently bereaved brother, Clarence. Such a match, she hoped, would push Edward into closer alliance with Burgundy. Clarence was undoubtedly attracted by the wealth of the Duchess; however there was a further reason for his interest. He had once been Warwick's favoured candidate for the English throne, and under the later agreement with Warwick would have succeeded to throne, since Edward, Henry's son had died without issue. He regarded the marriage as way of re-establishing his influence and perhaps of providing an alternative means of attaining the English kingship.

Despite his hopes, fortune frowned on Clarence as he suffered a further series of humiliations, for not only did Edward, being aware of the danger, forbid the marriage, but Mary was herself by no means inclined to accept him. Edward finally supported Mary's choice: the son of the Holy Roman Emperor, Maximilian of Austria. Furthermore, Clarence was cognisant that Edward had also put forward Earl Rivers as a suitable match, a clear insult since he was a member of no great family and was a Woodville to boot. It was no consolation that Edward, under pressure to satisfy Elizabeth's ambitions for her family, had made this proposal without entertaining any realistic hopes for its acceptance. The Croyland chronicler reported on the growing rift between Edward and Clarence.[37]

> *The indignation of the Duke was probably still increased by this [Mary's marriage]; and now each began to look upon each other with no very fraternal eyes. You might have then seen (as such men are generally to be found in the courts of all princes), flatterers running to and fro, from the one side to the other, and carrying backwards and forwards the words which had fallen from the two brothers, even if they had happened to be spoken in the most secret closet.*

Then Clarence, rather the victim of his own ambition and foolishness than the dupe of fortune, hastened his own downfall. At a Council meeting, he tried to argue the innocence of Thomas Burdett, one of his followers, sentenced to death for treason and necromancy, by having a cleric, notable for his support of Henry VI, read out a defence. Another associate of Clarence, whom he sought to defend, John Stacey, was also executed on a charge of necromancy. There is a suggestion that Clarence was the victim of a carefully contrived plan, conceived by the Woodvilles to trap him by means of attacking his supporters, for it was hoped that if he failed to speak up for them he would be dishonoured, while a passionate defence of these men convicted of treason would further discredit him in the eyes of the king. Then there were whispers that he was reiterating rumours of Edward's illegitimacy and also reports reached Edward that Clarence was employing sorcery and had fomented the disturbances in Cambridgeshire and Huntingdonshire. However, it was only after he had summarily executed Ankarette Twynho on a charge of poisoning her mistress that Edward finally lost patience and had him imprisoned in the Tower in May 1477 for usurping the king's authority. Yet Mancini, at least, was suspicious of the charges laid against him and considered that he might have been the victim of a false rumour - the more easily believed, given his past conduct.

> *Accordingly, whether the charge was fabricated, or a real plot revealed, the Duke of Clarence was accused of conspiring the king's death by spells and magicians.*

Mancini goes on to suggest that Elizabeth was behind Clarence's downfall for she had *"concluded that her offspring by the king would never come to the throne unless the Duke of Clarence were removed; and of this she easily persuaded the king"*.

It may be that the delay in calling Parliament to pass the bill of attainder in January 1478 was owing to Edward's reluctance to execute his brother; Edward was perhaps also aware that it would appear to give the unpopular Woodvilles another victory. Richard made his support for Clarence obvious, but the trial proceeded, and Clarence was indicted and convicted on the grounds that he *"had falsely and traitorously intended and purposed firmly the extreme destruction and disinheriting of the King and his issue"* and possibly that he had claimed that the king was illegitimate. There were, however, also those rumours that had now come to the notice of the Woodvilles suggesting that Clarence had questioned the validity of Edward's marriage to Elizabeth. Thus, although Clarence no longer posed any real military threat to Edward, the rumours were very damaging. If Edward's marriage were invalid, that would place Clarence next in line of succession, and if Edward himself were illegitimate, Clarence would be the rightful king. These claims did not die with Clarence, for they were to re-emerge after Edward's death with important consequences. Edward, perhaps somewhat unwillingly and almost certainly under pressure from the Woodvilles, was finally persuaded to carry out the execution at the insistence of parliament on 18 February 1478. There is good evidence that he was executed in a most unusual way, being drowned in a butt of malmsey wine. Mancini reports that *"The mode of execution preferred in this case was that he should die by being plunged into a jar of sweet wine"*.[38] However, de Commines, Vergil and the *Great Chronicle of London* mention malmsey specifically. Perhaps the choice of drowning in wine was Clarence's own choice, a view supported by the evidence of his daughter wearing a bracelet depicting a miniature cask of wine.

Rous believed that superstition played a part in Clarence's execution.[39]

> *And because there was a certain prophecy that after E. – that is, after Edward IV, - G. should reign, for this ambiguity George Duke of Clarence, who was the middle brother between Edward and Richard, was killed on account of his name of George. And the other G., that is Gloucester lived to fulfil the prophecy.*

Vergil reported the same rumour, and Mancini described what happened next.[40]

> *At that time Richard Duke of Gloucester was so overcome with grief for his brother that he could not dissimulate so well, but that he was overheard to say that he would one day avenge his brother's death.*
>
> *Thenceforth he came very rarely to court. He kept himself within his own lands and set out to acquire the loyalty of his people through*

favours and justice. The good reputation of his private life and public activities powerfully attracted the esteem of strangers...Richard acquired the favour of the people, and avoided the jealousy of the queen from whom he lived far separated.

After the execution of the Duke of Clarence, and while Richard [kept] himself to his own lands, the queen ennobled many of her family. Besides she attracted to her party many strangers and introduced them to court, so that they alone should manage the public and private business of the crown, surround the king, and have bands of retainers, give or sell offices and finally rule the very king himself...

Richard's absence, such as it was - for he did not cut himself entirely off from court life, attending the wedding of his nephew Richard in 1478 and having his name appear on all the royal charters from February 1478 to 1483 (showing that he was at least kept informed of events) - was as much to do with his anger at the death of Clarence and the Woodville influence that had brought it about, as his fear. Although he had been demonstrably loyal to Edward, who was to say that the Woodvilles whom he was powerless to challenge, might not also consider him a threat in need of removal. He could, however, strengthen his position by consolidating his power in the north.

Thomas More, for whom any stick was good with which to beat the reputation of Richard, perversely, and apparently with no supporting evidence - as he admits - managed to turn Richard's brave defence of Clarence against him.[41]

Somme wise menne also weene [believe], that his drifte couertly conuayd, lacked not in helping furth his brother Clarence to his death: which hee resisted openly, howbeit somewhat (as menne demed) more faintly than that he wer hartely minded to his welth [welfare]. And they that thus deme, think that he long time in Edwardes life forethought to be king in case that the king his brother (whose life hee looked that euil dyete shoulde shorten) shoulde happen to decease (as in dede he did) while his children were yonge. And thei deme, that for thys intente he was gladde of his brothers death the Duke of Clarence, whose life must needes haue hindered hym so entendynge, whither the same Duke of Clarence hadde kepte him true to his nephew the yonge king, or enterprised to be king himself. But of al this point is there no certaintie and whoso diuineth vppon conjectures maye as wel shote to farre as to short.

Thomas More

Audiences familiar with Shakespeare's Richard III will be aware of the calumny.

There is no doubt that Richard did benefit from Clarence's disgrace and execution, for he took Clarence's share of Barnard Castle and regained the office of great chamberlain of England which he had previously had to surrender to him. Additionally, three days before Clarence's death, Richard's son was granted the title of Earl of Salisbury, one Clarence's titles. Nevertheless, Richard's good fortune provides no evidence of his guilt.

Edward's reluctance to execute Clarence, as recorded by Vergil, would seem to be indicated by his regret at his death, adding support to the view that he was persuaded to this course by the Woodvilles.[42]

> *But yt ys very lykly that king Edward right soone repentyd that dede; for he was woont to cry owt in a rage, "O infortunate brother, for whose lyfe no man in this world wold once make request;" affirming in that manyfestly, that he was cast away by the envy of the nobylytie.*

The belligerent instincts of Richard on the English side and the Duke of Albany on the Scottish helped to restart the war between the two countries in 1480, thus destroying what peace had existed since the treaty of 1474. Richard, in addition to his existing position as Warden of the West Matches of Scotland, was appointed Lieutenant in the North, and, with Edward reluctantly supporting Richard's aggressive stance, it was expected that the two brothers would lead a campaign against the Scots in 1481. However, although Scottish shipping was severely disrupted by a naval campaign in the Forth, Edward remained in the south, perhaps by reason of ill-health. Louis, perceiving a means by which he might avoid making his payments to Edward, encouraged the Scots in their belligerence. Richard then, supported by Percy, and with about 20,000 men at his command committed himself to the campaign he had long desired.

In 1481 Richard and Percy attacked and besieged Berwick, but a threat to Percy's own lands forced a withdrawal. Then in 1482, the Duke of Albany, who was prepared to sacrifice his lands in the south west of Scotland in hope of taking the crown for himself, an ambition he long entertained, threw his support behind Richard. But when Albany proved unreliable funds were insufficient to prolong the campaign and Richard withdrew, capturing Berwick on 24 August.

Typically hostile to Richard, the Croyland Chronicler complained about the expense and futility of the campaign.[43]

> *At this time and during nearly two years before the king's death, King Louis failed in the strict observance of the engagements which he had previously entered into as to the truce and tribute; as he was only watching for a time at which he might be released from all fears of the English. For after the agreement had become generally known, which had been made with the people of Flanders, and by which the daughter of Duke Maximilian was to be given in marriage to the Dauphin, the king was defrauded of one year's tribute; while in the meantime, captures began to take place, both of subjects and ships of the two kingdoms. Amid these tempests in which the English were thus involved, the Scots, encouraged by the French, of whom they had been allies of old, imprudently broke the treaty of peace for thirty years which we had formerly made with them; and this, notwithstanding the fact that king Edward had long paid a yearly sum of one thousand marks by way of dowry for Cecily, one of his daughters, who had been promised in marriage by a formal embassy to the eldest son of the king of the Scots. In consequence of this, a tremendous and destructive war was proclaimed by Edward against the Scots, and the entire command of the expedition was given to Richard, duke of Gloucester, the king's brother.*
>
> *What he effected in this expedition, what sums of money, again extorted under the name of benevolences, he uselessly squandered away, the affair in its results sufficiently proved. For no resistance being offered, he marched as far as Edinburgh with the whole of his army, and then leaving that opulent city untouched, returned by way of Berwick, which town had been taken upon his first entrance into that country; upon which, the castle, which held out much longer, not without vast slaughter and bloodshed, fell into the hands of the*

> *English. This trifling, I really know not whether to call it 'gain' or 'loss' (for the safe keeping of Berwick each year swallows up ten thousand marks), at this period diminished the resources of king and kingdom by more than a hundred thousand pounds. King Edward was vexed at this frivolous outlay of so much money, although the recovery of Berwick above-mentioned in some degree alleviated his sorrow. These were the results of the duke's expedition into Scotland in the summer of the year of our Lord, 1482, the same being the twenty-second of the reign of king Edward.*

Although the identity of the Croyland chronicler remains a mystery, his obvious southern sympathies make him naturally antagonistic towards Richard.

Vergil put it a little differently.[44]

> *The duke of Glocester, entring Scotland, wastyd and burnyd all over the countrie, and, marching further into the land, encampyd himself nor farre from his enemyes; whan as, perceiving that not one man of all the Scottishe nation resortyd to the duke of Albany, he suspected treason, not without cause; wherof he tooke treuce with king James, and returnyd the right way to Berwicke, whiche in the meane time Thomas lord Stanley had woone, without losse of many his men. And King James, whose subjects bare him no good will, was forcyd by nesitie, after treuce taken, to digest that displeasure of winning the towne. The duke of Albany, repenting afterward that he had bene the author of that war, wherby both his country and himself was annoyed, and, seeing himselfe in no reputation emonest thigloishe men, departyd into France, wher not long after he was killyd in running at tylt.*

There is no firm evidence that Edward was displeased with Richard's efforts and, although an open show of support might cover private exasperation, he publicly praised his brother, recognising the advantages of the capture of Berwick, a strategically important town, since its removal from Scots' hands severely restricted their ability to launch attacks down the east coast. In his letter to Pope Sixtus IV Edward showed his pride in Richard's achievements.[45]

> ...the army which our brother lately led into Scotland, traversing the heart of that kingdom without hindrance, arrived at the royal city of Edinburgh, and found the King with the other chief lords of the kingdom shut up in a most strongly fortified castle, nowise thinking of arms, of war, of resistance, but giving that right fair and opulent city into the power of the English, who, had not their compassion exceeded all human cupidity, would have instantly doomed the same to plunder and the flames. The noble band of victors, however, spared the supplicant and prostrate citizens, the churches, and not only the widows and orphans, and minors, but all persons found there unarmed. To this favour there contributed the intercession of the Duke of Albany, who of late years having been undeservedly banished by his brother the King of Scots, and now by our power restored to his estates and titles, was of the opinion that his return would be the more welcome if our soldiers, for his sake, modified the contributions levied by them on the country.
>
> The chief advantage of the whole expedition is the reconquest of the town and castle of Berwick...

Although an element of flattery must be taken into consideration, Parliament applauded Richard's successes, even if there is perhaps a hint that he was expected to achieve a little more.

Undoubtedly the campaign served Richard's purposes well, even if it had not been the glittering military success he might wished. Not only had he achieved a measure of protection from Scottish raids for his people and lands, but had secured for himself autonomous rule, by being granted a palatinate in Scotland over the lands conquered by him and heirs. Furthermore, he was created sheriff of Cumberland, and his Wardenship of the West Marches, which had been merely a life interest, was granted as a hereditary interest. Richard must have found great satisfaction in gaining such a measure of independence from Edward, and, with some of the security he constantly sought having been achieved, could look forward to establishing his power on an ever-firmer footing.

However, Edward's resources and attention (such as it was) being taken by the Scottish war, a war contrary to his political instincts, might have allowed a serious political problem to develop. In 1482 Louis signed a treaty with the Emperor Maximilian, who was married to Mary of Burgundy, including a provision to betroth the dauphin to Maximilian's three-year-old daughter. This was not only a humiliation for Edward, since it broke the agreement in the Treaty of Piquigny by which the dauphin was to marry Edward's daughter, but it also removed the possibility of Edward ever receiving the payments which were to have begun at the consummation of the marriage, and, worst of all, it brought about an alliance of France and Burgundy, isolating England, a situation Edward had striven to avoid for many years. The scheming Louis had won a decisive political victory over the increasingly indolent and pleasure-seeking Edward, reducing his foreign policy to tatters.

On 9 April 1483 Edward IV died unexpectedly at the comparatively early age of forty. It was reported that he died of a chill caught during a boating expedition on the Thames, though his licentious and dissolute lifestyle may also have been a contributory factor. Edward had consolidated his hold on power by entrusting the government of the further flung reaches of his kingdom to those whom he felt he could trust. However, this policy produced mixed results, for although Richard had proved an able and reliable lord in the north, Clarence, who had been given control of the West Country had proved to be treacherous. The legacy of the Woodville problem was to continue beyond Edward's death with more disastrous consequences. Edward had left the Woodvilles in a powerful position, but it was not completely secure from attack, for to consolidate their power the Woodvilles needed to keep Edward's sons safe and to maintain their influence over them, especially the twelve year old Edward. Their rise to power during the reign of

Edward had not been accompanied by a corresponding acceptance of their new prominence, being disliked and distrusted by many, and the antagonism they provoked was to be their undoing.

And so Edward passed, a king charismatic and vigorous at the beginning of his reign, but lax and licentious by the end; on the one hand brave in battle and politically aware, on the other lacking determination and commitment in administration; more interested in pleasure and the trappings of kingship than in governing his realm with energy and wisdom; who fought bloody wars to establish a dynasty, yet who died having failed to secure the safe succession of his son. He was a man possessed of many gifts, a ruler who might have achieved true greatness, but who, by indulging his desires and neglecting his duty, squandered what advantages he had been given, resurrecting the very thing his bloody battles against the Lancastrians, ruthless seizing of the crown and determination not to yield his sceptre to rebels seemed to have eradicated: political instability.

-4-

Appearance and Character

The suggestion that the murky arts of propaganda played their part in the artistic portrayal of Richard have created an interest in his appearance far beyond that engendered by most historical characters, since a distortion of his appearance could be taken as indicative of a broader Tudor policy, all too-understandable, given Henry VII's lack of a legitimate claim to the throne, to malign the personality and actions of the king who had been usurped.

The alterations apparent in some of Richard's portraits and the contradictory descriptions given of his appearance provoked Ricardians to identify a Tudor desire to present physical deformities in Richard that could be taken as mirroring moral deformities. Before considering how recent discoveries might have altered the position it is worthwhile to examine how the arguments were presented.

Many will be familiar with Shakespeare's description of a *"bottled spider"* and a *"poisonous, hunchbacked, toad"* with a withered arm, a king whose physical appearance was so allied to his malignity that he could be presented as a fiend lurching across the stage to infest the fearful corners of the imagination. Such a description was sanctioned by some contemporary and near contemporary accounts.

William Burton of York, a drunken schoolmaster, writing in 1491, six years after Richard's death, said that he *"was a hypocrite, a crook back [and] was buried in a dyke like a dog"*. However, since Burton incorrectly describes Richard's burial, we can place no confidence in the rest of his description. The problems of the bias in the writers and the reliability of their accounts are of particular importance and difficulty in the case of Richard and ones that will encountered again and again.

Rous, a chantry priest, who at the time was residing in Warwickshire, wrote his *History of the Kings of England*, dedicated in flattering terms to Henry VII, and containing a description of Richard, for John Seymour, who was considering subjects for the statues to fill the niches in St George's Chapel.[1]

> *Richard was born at Fotheringhay in Northamptonshire, retained within his mother's womb for two years and emerging with teeth and hair to his shoulders...At his nativity Scorpio* was in the ascendant...And like a scorpion he combined a smooth front with a stinging tail. He received his lord King Edward V blandly, with embraces and kisses, and within about three months, or a little more he killed him together with his brother, And Lady Anne, his queen, daughter of the Earl of Warwick, he poisoned...And what was most detestable to God and to all Englishmen, and indeed to all nations to whom it became known, he caused others to kill the holy man King Henry VI, or as many think, did so by his own hands...He was small of stature, with a short face and unequal shoulders, the right higher and the left lower...*
>
> *This King Richard, who was excessively cruel in his days, reigned for three years and a little more, in the way that Antichrist is to reign. And like the Antichrist to come, he was confounded at his moment of greatest pride.*

(*Although Richard's birth date is not currently assigned to Scorpio, it seems that October as a whole could be taken as being under the influence of that sign.)

Such a description might be considered almost conclusively damning were it not for its obvious exaggerations concerning Richard's birth and for the fact that Rous had earlier, during the Richard's life, written about in him in the most laudatory terms, including two drawings showing no deformity.[2]

> *The most mighty Prince Richard...all avarice set aside ruled his subjects in his realm most commendably, punishing offenders of his laws, especially extortioners and oppressors of his commons, and cherishing those that were virtuous, by which the discreet guiding he got great thanks of God and love of all his subjects, rich and poor, and great praise of the people of all other lands about him.*

Moreover, another illustration of Richard in the Latin version of Rous's later Tudor version also lacks any hint of deformity. The inaccuracies in Rous's other work make it difficult to place much reliance on his writing.

Thomas More, an important and influential figure and friend of Henry VIII wrote an unfinished history of Richard in English and Latin. The reader can almost feel his delight in creating a villainous character.[3]

> *Richarde the third sonne of whom we nowe entreate, was in witte and courage egal with either of them [Edward and George], in bodye and prowesse farre vnder them bothe, little of stature, ill fetured of limnes, croke backed, his left shoulder much higher than his right, hard fauoured of visage, and suche as is in states called warlye, in other menne otherwise, he was malicious, wrathfull, enuious and, from afrore his birth, euer frowarde. It is for trouth reported that the Duches his mother had muche adoe in her trauaile, [from the Latin version, and other editions – "that she could not be delivered of him uncut"] and that hee came into the world with feete forwarde, as menne bee borne outwarde, and (as the fame runneth) also not vntothed, whither menne of hatred reporte aboue the trouthe, or elles that nature changed her course in hys beginninge, whiche in the course of his lyfe many thinges vnnaturallye committed...He was close and secrete, a deepe dissimuler, lowlye of counteynaunce, arrogant of heart, outwardly coumpinable where he inwardely hated,*

> *not letting to kisse whome hee thought to kyll; dispitious and cruell, not for euill will always, but ofter for ambicion, and either for the suretie or encrease of his estate. Frende and foo was muche what indifferent, where his aduauntage grew, he spared no mans deathe, whose life withstood his purpose.*

Morton, an enemy of Richard, was probably his main source, since More had served as a page in Morton's house and was closely connected to him. If this was the case, More certainly had access to first-hand information about certain parts of Richard's life, and his account as a whole is likely to contain the basis of what actually happened, for there were enough people still living at the time of writing who would also be able to recall these events and to comment on their veracity. But More's additions and interpretations make it difficult for us to place too much confidence in what he writes, especially where Morton would be able to provide no personal account. More also has Richard's left shoulder higher than the right, contrary to other descriptions. Another reason to doubt the veracity of More is that he describes Richard as having been born by caesarean section. The earliest example of a woman surviving such a procedure is not otherwise found until the 1580s in Siegershausen. Richard's mother, Cecily, survived the birth, living until 1495.

Polydore Vergil gives an almost equally hostile description.[4]

> *He raigned two yeres and so many monethes, and one day over. He was lyttle of stature, deformyd of body, thone showlder being higher than thother, a short and sowre cowntenance, which semyd to savor of mischief, and utter evydently craft and deceyt. The whyle he was thinking of any matter, he dyd contynually byte his nether lyppe, as howgh that crewell nature of his did so rage agaynst yt self in that lyttle carkase. Also he was woont to be ever with his right hand pulling out of the sheath to the myddest, and putting in agane, the dagger which he did alway were. Trewly he had a sharp witt, provydent and subtyle, apt both to counterfayt and dissemble; his*

corage also hault and fearce, which faylyd him not in the very death, which, whan his men forsooke him, he rather yealded to take with the swoord, than by fowle flyght to prolong his lyfe, uncertane what death perchance soon after by sicknes or other vyolence to suffer.

Vergil, sometimes named *The Father of English History*, has claim to be the first true historian of England, yet his accounts of Richard cannot be taken at face value. Later in his history he will give the wrong year for Buckingham's rebellion, not the only date error in his work, and he was, if not completely beholden to Henry VII, at least aware that in order to provide some justification for Henry's invasion and usurpation of the throne, the House of Plantagenet, as represented by its last king, had to be denigrated. Yet as with all those early chroniclers and writers recording events and commenting on Richard's life, it is not enough simply to dismiss their narratives and explanations. They deserve more careful scrutiny. Although Vergil wrote his *English History* at the request of Henry VII, he was an honest enough historian to consult a number of sources, including those men who had lived through the events of Richard's reign, and to make some comments favourable to Richard. He did not feel constrained, however, from biasing his account against Richard, especially when surmising his motives.

By the seventeenth century, the established Tudor portrayal had been embellished with further derogatory descriptions, so that Baker in his *Chronicle of the Kings of England*, 1643, could describe Richard in luridly hostile terms.

There never was in any Man a greater Uniformity of Body and Mind, than was in him; both of them equally deformed. Of body he was but low, Crook-back'd, Hook-shoulderd, Splay-footed, and Goggle-eyed; his face little and round, his Complexion swarthy, his left Arm from his Birth dry and withered; born a Monster in Nature, with all his Teeth, with Hair on his Head and Nails on his Fingers and Toes: And just such were the Qualities of his Mind. One Quality he had in ordinary, which was, to look fawningly when he plotted, sternly when he executed. Those Vices, which in other Men are Passions, in him were Habits; and his Cruelty was not upon Occasion, but natural. If at any Time he shewed any Virtue, it was Pretence; the Truth of his Mind was only Lying and Falsehood. He was full of Courage, and yet not valiant, Valour consisting not only in doing, but as well in suffering, which he could not abide. He was politick, and yet not wise; Policy looking to the Middle, Wisdom to the End, which he did and did not. It was not so much Ambition that made him desire the Crown as Cruelty; that it might be within his Power to kill at his Pleasure: And to say the Truth, he was scarce of the Number of Men who consist of Flesh and Blood, being nothing but Blood. One Miracle we say he did; which was, that he made the Truth of History to exceed the Fiction of Poetry, being a greater Harpy than those that were feigned. He would fain have been accounted a good King, but for his Life he could not be a good Man; and it is an impossible Thing to be one without the other. He left no Issue behind him: And had it been Pity he should, at least in his own Image; one such Monster was enough for many Ages.

The painting of Richard III in the Royal Collection, dating to about 1520, probably a copy of an earlier portrait, clearly shows the right shoulder higher than the left, seemingly confirming some of the descriptions. However, close examination, supported by an x-ray photograph, reveals that the picture was altered after it was originally painted to raise the shoulder, narrow the right eye and perhaps to enlarge the nose and thin the lips. Ricardians took this as evidence of Tudor propaganda which aimed to legitimise Henry VII's usurpation and denigrate the memory of Richard, especially since a portrait in possession of the Royal Society of Antiquaries shows no deformity of the shoulders, although it too shows evidence of alteration to the mouth. Dr Tudor Craig in a catalogue to the 1973 exhibition argued that the portrait in the Royal Collection provided the model for all the versions that followed, including the portrait in the National Gallery.

Richard III (The Royal Collection)

Suspicions that the Tudors had employed propaganda systemically and ruthlessly to destroy Richard's reputation were increased, because some other visual depictions fail to reveal the deformity of the shoulders, mention of which is similarly absent in the descriptions of other writers of the time, who sometimes even remark on his good looks and note his virtues.

An illustration in *Quinte Curse Ruffe des fais du Grand Alexandre* showing a man wearing the Order of the Garter, which may be a representation of Richard, and a drawing of Richard in *The Pageant of Richard Beauchamp – Earl of Warwick* both depict a man without deformities.

Nicholas von Poppelau, a knight visiting from Bohemia in 1484 made no mention of a hunchback, noting that Richard was about two inches taller than himself, but slimmer and that he *"had delicate arms and legs"*, though, since there is no indication of von Poppelau's stature, this gives us little indication of Richard's height.

The Croyland chronicler, Fabian (in the *Great Chronicle of London*), Mancini, and Commines, all to some degree hostile to Richard, fail to mention any deformity. When Fabian describes the treatment of Richard's body after Bosworth, perhaps a description of his deformity might have been expected but is absent.[5]

> *And Richard late king, [his] body despoiled to the skin and nought being left about him so much as would cover his privy member, was trussed behind a pursuivant called Norroy as a hog or other vile beast, and so, all bespattered with mire and filth, was brought to a church in Leicester for all men to wonder upon and there lastly irreverently buried.*

Archibald Whitelaw who was a member of the King of Scotland's council and an envoy to the English court made a formal oration to Richard on 12 September 1484.[6]

> *Most serene Prince and King; of all the sovereigns whom I have known, you stand out as the greatest – in the renown of your nobility, in your sway over your people, in your strength of arms, and in the wealth of resources at every form of virtue (has) reached into every corner of the world; moreover, there is the excellent and outstanding humanity of you innate benevolence, your clemency, your liberality, your good faith, your supreme justice, and your incredible greatness of heart. Your wisdom is not just human, it is almost divine: for you make yourself not simply at ease with important individuals, but courteous to the common people too…(Now) I look for the first time upon your face; it is a countenance worthy of the highest power and kingliness, illuminated by moral and heroic virtue. Fitting for you are the words which the poet Statius used of the noble prince of Thebes: "Never before has nature dared to encase in a smaller body such spirit and such strength…In his small body the greatest valour held sway." For you are the embodiment of military skill, prowess, good fortune and authority – all qualities which Cicero, in his eulogy of Pompey, declares should be sought in the best military leader…In you, however, most serene Prince, all the requirements of a glorious king and general come together…Were Cicero still alive, his skills would scarcely suffice to describe your virtues fully or sing your praises to the skies…*

However, since this was intended to be a formally flattering address we should not attach too much importance to its literal accuracy.

John Stow (1525-1605), an antiquarian, described Richard as *"of bodily shape comely enough only low of stature"*, while Horace Walpole claimed that *"the old Countess of Desmond who had danced with Richard declared that he was the handsomest man in the room except his brother Edward, and was very well made"*.[7]

Pietro Carmeliano, wrote of Richard in glowing terms in 1484.[8]

> *If we look [for] religious devotion, what prince is there in our time who shows a more genuine piety? If for justice, who can we reckon*

> *above him throughout the world? If we look for prudence in fostering peace and waging war, who shall we judge his equal? If we look for truth of soul, for wisdom, for loftiness of mind united with modesty, who stands before our King Richard? What Christian Emperor or Prince can be compared with him in good works and munificence? To whom are theft, rebellion, pollution, adultery, manslaughter, usury, heresy and abominable crimes more hateful than to him? Obviously, no one.*

Yet we cannot take this as a trustworthy description either, since, once Richard was dead, Carmeliano condemned him with equal spirit.

We can place more trust in the honesty and accuracy of Thomas Langton, Bishop of St David's, who was writing to the Prior of Christ Church in September 1483, as the letter was not a deliberate attempt at flattery.[9]

> *I trust to God soon, by Michaelmas, the king shall be in London. He contents the people wherever he goes better than ever did any prince; for many a poor man that has suffered wrong many days has been relieved and helped by him and his commands in his progress. And in many great cities and towns were great sums of money which were given to him which he has refused. On my faith I never liked the qualities of a prince as well as his. God has sent him to us for the welfare of us all.*

Certainly the city of York was convinced of his virtues as we have already seen.

The Ricardians, taking the doctored portrait as evidence of determined Tudor bias against Richard, treated many of the chroniclers with a degree of suspicion, being convinced that their accounts were likely to be equally as biased.

Then the discovery of Richard's bones in the car park in Leicester provided a crucial piece of evidence to help to settle at least one aspect of the long-running debate. It was found that he suffered from scoliosis of the spine, a condition that would have manifested itself when he was about ten years old, producing severe twisting of the vertebrae and abnormalities in their shape and, depending upon its severity, have made the right shoulder sit higher than the left. The clothing that Richard wore could have disguised some or all of the physical effects. The condition might, in addition have put pressure on his lungs causing shortness of breath, but he would have still been able to function as a battle commander.

The likelihood that Richard did indeed suffer from such a physical deformity has consequences for the interpretation placed upon the writings of Tudor chroniclers, for, if Richard's portrait was altered to adhere more closely to the physical truth, and was not merely an attempt to imply that his twisted body held a twisted mind, then perhaps these writers can be considered to have edged closer to the truth and to have been less influenced by a desire to pen derogatory propaganda than Ricardians would like to assume. However, this is only to say that their criticisms may not be too readily discounted, and not to pretend that their works are free from bias, prejudice and Tudor influences.

The question of Richard's personal piety is one that is likely to provide a sharp division of opinion, for if the assumption is that Richard was essentially a good king and that there is little or no justification for the crimes attributed to him, then he will appear a devout and God-fearing Catholic who promoted religion as a duty laid upon him, while if he is regarded as the evil perpetrator of hideous crimes, then the conclusion will be that he was a devious hypocrite, a further charge to add to the indictment drawn up against him.

We can but conjecture what the attitude of his mother, Cecily Neville, was to Richard's later claim to the throne but there is enough evidence to suggest that Richard remained on good terms with his her. Some time before Richard became Protector, after his visit to her at Syon, she wrote to him regretting that he was not able to visit her at Berkhamstead. Although Cecily, known for her religious observance, would not have had a direct influence on Richard's upbringing while he was beyond her supervision, certainly in those formative years he spent with her before being sent to the households of the Archbishop of Canterbury, Thomas Bourchier, and Warwick, it would be surprising if she had not begun to form Richard's religious outlook, or at least laid the foundations for his life as a Christian man.

Richard's books provide some evidence for his attitude towards his religious obligations. He owned the New Testament in Wycliffe's earlier literal English translation of the Latin Vulgate, an English paraphrase of the Old Testament, and the *Liber Specialis Gratiae* containing the mystical visions of Matilda of Hackenborn. Any suggestion that Richard had leanings towards the Lollards – a heretical sect sometimes regarded as proto-Protestants – has no foundation, since this version of Wycliffe was generally regarded as perfectly orthodox, despite the ban on unapproved translations dating from later than 1408. Richard's education had been disrupted owing to the wars and it is not possible to be sure how fully he understood Latin, but his possession of vernacular translations indicates his desire to be fully versed in Holy Scripture. The *Liber Specialis Gratiae* contains his wife's name, and it is not unreasonable to suppose that, even if the book was not Richard's own, he was familiar with it, especially since his mother owned a copy too. Many who could afford it, and were literate enough to read it, possessed a Book of Hours, which was essentially a shorter version of the Divine Offices sung in the monasteries and abbeys the length of Catholic Christendom. Much has been made of the prayer written for him with alterations, included in this book, which is a prayer for deliverance from afflictions, temptation, ill-health, danger and attacks from enemies. Yet this Biblically-based prayer seems to have been a conventional prayer, originating in the fourteenth century, not specifically composed for Richard, and found in the books of other rulers of the time, which is not say that he did not pray it piously in all seriousness and honesty.

Richard's other books included *De Regimine Principum* by Aegidius Colonna; Chaucer's *The Knight's Tale*; the *Destruction of Troy*; the *Siege of Thebes*; *Chronicle of English History*; and Geoffrey of Monmouth's *History*. It is not possible to say how far Richard followed the advice in these books about princely conduct, drew lessons from history, or whether indeed he read any of these books. It is, however, likely that he was familiar with the books' contents and that he had a fairly conventional education for a prince of his time.

The portrait of Richard in possession of the Royal Society of Antiquaries depicts Richard's devotion to the Blessed Virgin for he is wearing a symbol associated with her, a brooch in shape of a rose, a ruby set in gold surrounded by petals.

In assessing how far Richard had a genuine regard for religion his actions too ought to be taken into consideration. As Lord of Middelham, the Praemonstratensian Abbey at Coverham fell to his responsibility and he seems to have shown genuine concern for its situation, giving it grants of money.

> ...unto oure trusty and welbelovede in god Thabbot & Convent of Coverham xxli of money towards the belding their Churche an reperacione of other things necessarie within thaire place...

He also purchased and gave them the advowson of Seaham to supplement their income.

The great Minster at York benefitted from his generosity. He granted the patronage of Cottingham to provide an income supporting the Vicars Choral and had grand plans to establish a college of one hundred priests in a building that may well have been intended to be constructed adjacent to the Minster itself. This would have been a huge undertaking and immensely costly, not only in terms of the building project itself but also in providing sufficient income for such a large number of clergy and the necessary clerks, choristers and sacristans, to say nothing of the expenses of running and maintaining such a structure. His generosity to the Minster might not, however, have been completely disinterested for he probably intended that he would be buried in York and then his hugely impressive chantry church would be ready to welcome his body and to ease his soul's journey through the pains of purgatory with Masses and prayers. Undoubtedly he saw both the city of York and its Minster, the metropolitan cathedral of the north, as important in his efforts to secure his power and influence. The Minster, which attracted gifted and educated scholars and clergy could provide him with future supporters who would remember and repay his generosity and patronage. There is ample evidence that he did support the advancement of able man, men such as Thomas Barowe, John Doger, John Gunthorpe and the man whom he promoted to the See of Durham, John Shirwood.

Richard had plans to establish further chantries. A chantry at Barnard Castle was to be provided with twelve priests, ten clerks and six choristers and one clerk in order to pray for his family, while another was to be created at Middleham. However of the three, only the least ambitious, Middleham, in which it is clear from the statutes that he took particular interest, was ever completed. These statutes allowing for six priests, four clerks, six choristers and a clerk sacristan, gave instructions as to how the Divine Office (the daily round of services) should be celebrated and with what commemorations, with special celebrations for favoured saints. Interestingly he specified the Sarum Use for the Mass and Offices, rather than that of York, but this is not surprising, since the Use of York was confined to the Minster and relatively few parishes, while Sarum, the use with which Richard had probably grown up, was far more widespread and influential. This chantry was to pray for members of his family, living and dead, as well as all other Christian souls. He took particular care that the dean and other priests should be sufficiently skilled and learned. At least one of the clerks had to be highly proficient in all manner of music, good enough to be on a par with those at the most prestigious establishments – *"lerned in the practise of singing, aswel in playne song, priked song, fauburdon, counterpoint, descant of all measures used in any Cathedrall church or Collage"*. This clerk was to be master of choristers, responsible for their education and musical development. Once a boy's voice broke he was not to be deprived of his place immediately, but was to be allowed up to six months' grace, although presumably some of the most promising boys, as was the case elsewhere, could receive further training, perhaps even becoming priests of the college themselves. Richard's personal interest is attested by the provision that he had the sole right to revise the statutes.

Rous and Stow contend that he founded a further chantry at the church of St Mary Barking by the Tower (now All Hallows) but they might have mistaken this for a chantry established by Edward IV.

The Convocation of Canterbury wrote that he had *"a most noble and blessed disposition toward the Church"*.

Richard's interest in church music is evidenced not only by the Middleham statutes but also by Nicholas von Popplau, a noble, impressed by Richard, who wrote: *"The next day he went to mass and heard exquisite music in the church the king also attended"*. He also issued orders for impressing for his service both men and boy choristers from all other religious foundations except the Royal Chapel at Windsor, indicating that he took the choral aspect the services so seriously that he was prepared to remove the best singers from elsewhere in order to adorn his own chapel. Such powers of impressment, which strike us as being a manifestation of the overbearing presumption of royal power, were not unusual at this time and often provided a means of advancement for talented boys that would otherwise be denied.

Richard's concern for and generosity towards the Church needs to be understood in the context of the age. It was incumbent upon the powerful and wealthy to protect, promote and provide for the Church. Acts of generosity were not only expected of such princes as Richard, but were one of the ways in which the powerful men of the time could demonstrate their wealth and power; thus, while gaining merit with God, they extended their temporal influence over men. Yet Richard's munificence and interest perhaps reached beyond the normal bounds and indicate a man more than commonly aware of his obligations towards God and His Church. How far that awareness extended into the sphere of secular politics is another debate.

-5-

The Road to the Throne

When you play the game of thrones you win or you die [1]

The unexpectedly early death of the king, his brother, cast Richard into a storm of uncertainty. The dark ghosts of his turbulent childhood pushed away by his military triumphs and reputation, and by his increasing wealth and land holdings, threatened to advance across his life again. All was once more thrown into the hazard, and Richard feared that the political instabilities of his younger years had re-emerged with a power that could sweep away all the defences he had carefully built against them, even perhaps imagining the misery of imprisonment or executioner's sword prepared against his life and the lives of his wife and son. One clear threat came from the Woodvilles, who, advanced to power by the late king under the influence of his wife, backed by no ancient lineage and deeply resented by many, would not give up their grip on the government of the country without putting up determined resistance. The Wars of the Roses had taught the contenders for power an important lesson: *"When you play the game of thrones you win or you die"*.

Of course, in fifteenth century England many of those playing this game had no choice but to be contestants, their participation being decided by birth. One of these was Edward's eldest son, Prince Edward, who held court at Ludlow under the close control and supervision of the Woodvilles. He was under the protection of, Anthony, Earl Rivers, brother of the Elizabeth, who governed his household; another brother, Lionel, the Bishop of Salisbury acted as his chaplain; Sir Richard Grey, a son of an earlier marriage by Elizabeth controlled his accounts, assisted by her cousin, Richard Haute; and his master of horse was a brother of her previous husband. Anthony and Lionel acted as the prince's councillors.

Although the decision to place Edward with Rivers was no doubt influenced by Elizabeth's pressure, it was a sensible choice insofar that the scholarly Rivers could provide the young boy with the sort of education the king desired. In all likelihood, the prince would have been transferred to another household before he grew much older so that he could also be schooled in the arts of war and government. However, the king's final illness wrecked his plans, and realising that the power of the Woodvilles, and the youth of the prince with his lack of political and military inexperience posed dangers to the peace of the realm, he reversed the provision of his earlier will which had left his son to the care of Elizabeth, and directed that Richard should be protector both of the prince and of the realm. He gauged that the opposition to the Woodvilles would be met by their determination to keep a firm hold on power, resulting in further civil war. Thus, the reasons for placing the prince under Richard's guardianship were threefold: to remove the boy from the Woodvilles in order to prevent them legitimatising and consolidating their political control; to avoid the conflict that would follow a Woodville attempt to seize such control; and to provide his son with the guidance of a more politically adept, practical and military man. Although the later will has disappeared, Mancini noted that *"Edward in his will"* had directed that Richard *"should govern"*, while Rous asserted that Richard was *"brother of the dead king, and by his ordinance protector of England"*. Yet both Richard and the Woodvilles were aware that the actual possession of power is far more important than any piece of paper purporting to confer it.

Perhaps to gain time, or perhaps because he was as yet undecided, Richard *"wrote the most soothing letters to console the queen"*; he promised to come and offer submission, fealty and all that was due from him to his lord and king, Edward V; and he was the first to swear an oath of fealty to the new king in York Minster.[2] It is, of course, possible that Richard was merely providing a cover for cruel ambition, though it is more likely that, being unprepared for the king's death, he was uncertain about the best course of action to follow and considered that by hiding any concerns he may have had for the prince he might avoid provoking precipitate action by the Woodvilles. Two powerful lords, Buckingham and Hastings allied themselves to Richard, and, though it is unclear how far Richard courted their friendship, they possessed reasons enough to dislike the Woodvilles and to seek a way of improving their lot. Buckingham nursed a long-held grievance for, having been a ward of Elizabeth from the age of nine, he had at eleven been forced to suffer the social humiliation of marriage to her sister, whose family were markedly his social inferiors.[3] His resentment was increased by what he saw as his deliberate exclusion from power under Edward. Hastings wielded power enough in Edward's administration, being household chamberlain, but he harboured a dislike of Thomas Grey, the queen's son by a previous marriage, and although Edward endeavoured resolve the matter by a show of reconciliation, in the end it was to no avail.

Elizabeth, understanding the antagonism she and the rest of the Woodvilles had created, knew that she was in danger from powerful lords who wished to strip her of her power, and having achieved that would be unlikely to allow her to continue as a threat. It was of the greatest importance that she should take control of the young king, for without him everything would be lost. Accordingly, while still having a majority on the council, before the arrival of Richard and other important lords, the Woodville faction managed to pass a resolution depriving Richard of his protectorate and placing him instead at the head of an interim council.

The Woodvilles were mistaken in believing that, following the example of the council who had removed Duke Humphrey as sole protector of Henry VI, Richard could legitimately be removed from his position by such means, for in his case parliamentary approval was lacking and the two protectorates were dissimilar. Besides, constitutionally, if a protector functioned merely on the mandate of the council, there was little point in making provision for one, since in theory any council could always replace, and therefore, control a protector, thus negating the one important reason for providing one: to place a young king beyond the grasp of the scheming, the avaricious, the foolish and the ambitious. However, legitimate methods could be ignored when, as the Woodvilles understood, *de facto* trumped *de jure* power. Indeed, the Woodvilles had already exercised power illegitimately, for Mancini relates that Rivers had appointed Dorset deputy constable of the Tower without the required authority; and so the Woodvilles were able to take possession of the armoury and to divide the treasure secured in the Tower between Elizabeth and her brother Sir Edward Woodville.

Thus, the Woodvilles hoped to hurry Edward from Ludlow and crown him in haste, since being a crowned monarch, even if still a boy, he would have greater influence, an influence that would undoubtedly help to secure their positions and exclude Richard. The coronation was set for the earliest possible date, 4 May, just under a month since Edward's death. He was another one of those unfortunate boys, along with his younger brother Richard, caught in the powerlessness of childhood, whose lives were blasted by the conflicts that recked neither age nor innocence.

Given the circumstances, Richard could hardly fail to acknowledge the threat the Woodvilles posed him and he too was eventually enmeshed once more, probably against his will, in that deadly game of thrones.

The *Croyland Chronicle* reports that Hastings also felt threatened by the Woodvilles.[4]

> *For he was afraid lest, if the supreme power should fall into the hands of the queen's relations, they would enact a most signal vengeance for the injuries which had been inflicted on them by that same lord; in consequence of which there had long existed extreme ill-will between the said lord Hastings and them.*

It is likely, therefore, that Hastings was one of the leaders of the group who opposed the queen in the council; and Mancini wrote *"it was the common report"* that he sent messengers and letters to Richard urging him to march south, although, whatever Richard's plans were at this time, he seems to have understood that Richard would take the prince into his protection, away from the Woodville influence, until the time came for him to rule in his own right.

He secretly planned to provide Richard with the opportunity to wrest the prince away from the Woodvilles and so by the threat of withdrawing from the court and establishing himself in his stronghold in Calais, where he was governor, he persuaded the queen to write to Edward proposing that he should not *"exceed an escort of two thousand men"* when he came to London so as avoid provoking unrest. The queen could ill-afford to lose the powerful influence of Hastings, who would be effectively unassailable in Calais, and perhaps a future threat.[5] The logic of Hastings' proposal appeared sound, yet with the young king attended by such a comparatively small number, it would be easier for Richard to muster sufficient men to overpower them and take him into his own protection. Whether or not Elizabeth was aware of Hasting's real motive, she had no option but to proceed with her plan to bring her son to London with all haste for his coronation.

There is no evidence that at this time Richard planned on seizing the throne, rather he seems to have been driven both by his loyalty to his brother's wish that his son be guarded by his protectorate and by the necessity to protect himself from the Woodvilles, both aims requiring that the queen should be prevented from gaining control of her son. The only safe way to prevent the queen from doing so was to intercept the boy on his journey south and to place him under his own care. It is easy to see why Richard, plagued by fear of insecurity, prompted by a nature bent towards action and so unwilling to calculate consequences, should have adopted this course. But perhaps there was little else he could have done, though, his failure to consider what he would do once the boy was under his control created further problems.

Rivers having met messengers carrying Richard's offer to

accompany the king to London, agreed to meet him and Buckingham at Northampton on 29 April. However, when Richard arrived at Northampton, he discovered that Rivers, who had delayed setting out, had travelled on to Stony Stratford. Perhaps he was urged on by the need to press on to London for the planned coronation, or perhaps it was part of a plan to delay Richard while the king was hurried on ahead.

Rivers, the king's uncle, and Grey, his half-brother, rode to Northampton, ostensibly to explain the failed rendezvous. Richard entertained them at Stony Stratford, later being joined by Buckingham, and it was agreed that Rivers would stay in Northampton, riding together with Richard to Northampton in the morning to accompany the king on his ride south. However, the next morning, Richard, having taken possession of the keys of the inn, arrested Rivers and Grey before he and Buckingham, setting guards on the road to prevent news of the morning's events reaching the king's retinue, rode to Stony Stratford where it seemed that the king's company was already making preparations for departure. Richard informed the king that his relatives had conceived a plot to usurp the government by force, and although the boy burst into tears, evidence of such a plot was provided later when the dukes on the way to London discovered *"barrels of harness [military equipment]* in the possession of his escort. An account is provided by Mancini.[6]

> *Wherefore they reached the young king ignorant of the arrest and deprived of his soldiers, and immediately saluted him as their sovereign. Then they exhibited a mournful countenance, while expressing profound grief for the death of the king's father whose demise they imputed to his ministers as being such that that they had but little regard for his honour, since they were accounted the companions and servants of his vices, and had ruined his health. Wherefore, lest they play the same old game with the son, the dukes said these ministers should be removed from the king's side, because such a child would be incapable of governing so great a realm by means of puny men. Besides Gloucester himself accused them of*

conspiring his death and of preparing ambushes in the capital and on the road, which had been revealed to them by their accomplices. Indeed he said it was common knowledge that they had attempted to deprive him of the office of regent conferred on him by his brother. Finally, he decided that these ministers should be utterly removed for the sake of his own security, lest he fell into the hands of desperate men, who from their previous licence would be ready to dare anything. He said that he himself, who the king's father had approved, could better discharge all the duties of government, not only because of his experience of affairs, but also on account of his popularity. He would neglect nothing pertaining to the duty of a loyal subject and diligent protector. The youth, possessing the likeness of his father's noble spirit besides talent and remarkable learning, replied to this saying that he had merely had those ministers whom his father had given him; and relying on his father's prudence, he believed that good and faithful ones had been given to him. He had seen nothing evil in them and he wished to keep them unless otherwise proved to be evil. As for the government of the kingdom, he had complete confidence in the peers of the realm and the queen, so that this care but little concerned his former ministers. On hearing the queen's name the duke of Buckingham, who loathed her race, then answered, it was not the business of women but of men to govern kingdoms, and so if he cherished any confidence in her he had better relinquish it. Let him place all his hope in his barons, who excelled in nobility and power. Finally, the youth, perceiving their intention, surrendered himself to the care of his uncle, which was inevitable, for although the dukes cajoled him by moderation, yet they clearly showed that they were demanding rather than supplicating. Therefore on that same day the youth was taken to the very town where they had seized Lord Rivers. Of the king's attendants, or those who had come out to meet him, nearly all were ordered home. Richard, the queen's other son, who was quite young, and but little before had come from London to the king, was arrested with him in the same village, and with his brother, Richard was handed over to the care of guards in the same town.

Mancini's report gives the impression of relying on eye-witness account, yet there are problems with it. The replies of the king certainly seem like an elaboration, thoughtful and articulate beyond his years, and redolent of a narrator's bias. Besides, if Edward felt he could rely on his father's judgement in choosing *"good faithful"* ministers for him, surely he would also have relied on his father's choice of protector. It seems that Mancini wishes to imply the duplicity and hypocrisy of Richard, while emphasising the wisdom and powerlessness of the poor young boy who had fallen into his clutches. There is also a problem with the movement of Richard Duke of York; he can scarcely have been handed over to the guards if Elizabeth was to take him with her into sanctuary before Richard's arrival. No doubt, though, the gist of the story of Richard gaining control of Edward is correct; it is the details that are unreliable and that give an unfavourable picture of Richard compared with the child-king's *"noble spirit"*.

Rivers, Grey and Vaughan were sent north under guard to Pontefract, where they would later be executed.

Elizabeth had made her play and had lost. Realising the danger of such a defeat she hurried into the sanctuary at Westminster, taking with her Richard, Duke of York, her second son and her five daughters. Never one to concede easily when confronted by difficulties, she had a breach made in the walls through which her furniture could be carried. While it might be argued that Elizabeth was fearful of Richard's duplicity and viciousness, it is far more likely that she acted with instincts of a political realist. She had recognised the danger in not being able to take control of the boy king and by plotting against Richard she had brought even closer the peril she had sought to avert. Sanctuary provided a refuge in which she might play a longer game, for with her second son still in her care, all might not yet be lost, should anything happen to her elder son, or the balance of power begin to shift once more. There was potentially much to be gained by waiting.

Although some forces under the Marquis of Dorset tried to rally support for the queen in Westminster, the supporters of Richard and Buckingham gathered their forces in London and, Dorset, realising that public opinion ran strongly in favour Richard, gave up the fight and sought sanctuary with the queen. Sir Edward Woodville also fled, taking with him twenty ships and his share of the treasure looted from the Tower.

The Woodville faction was now confused and in disarray. The Archbishop of York, Rotherham, in a panic, surrendered the Great Seal to Elizabeth at the Tower, before realising the folly of this illegal act and ensuring it was returned. It was, however in vain for him to try to rescue the situation, for Richard, waiting in Northampton, perhaps to gauge opinion in London, having received news of Archbishop's foolishness, removed him from his position as Lord Chancellor and appointed Thomas Bourchier, Archbishop Canterbury, in his stead.

The unseemly haste with which the Woodvilles had contrived to hustle forward the coronation can be recognised as the political contrivance it was, since the boy reached London in the company of Richard and Buckingham on the same day as the proposed ceremony.

Mancini could not restrain himself from showing Richard's entry into London in a poor light.[7]

> *As these dukes were seeking at every turn to arouse hatred against the queen's kin, and to estrange public opinion from her relatives, they took special pains to do so on the day they entered the city. For ahead of the procession they sent four wagons loaded with weapons bearing the devices of the queen's brothers and sons.*

Mancini carefully ignores the fact that the Woodville faction was generally unpopular anyway and that Richard was merely showing the evidence of what he considered to be either a plot against himself, or one to take the control of the king away from him. And the reality of the age was that a man of Richard's rank who might be seen to pose a threat to a royal dynasty would always be mindful of the danger that he might be eliminated. As to the arms that Richard displayed, there can be no definite conclusions drawn. Mancini reports the outrage of many citizens at the possible plot, while others considered that the arms were for a

Scottish campaign. However, it is difficult to see why these arms would be stored so far from Scotland. Thomas More commented that the arms supposedly to be used to attack Richard on his way to London would have been more likely to have been on soldiers' backs than in barrels. Even if the arms were meant to equip a force larger than that actually provided for the king, there seems to be no satisfactory explanation for them being stored so far away from Ludlow where the king was resident unless they were to be collected by soldiers on the way to London to support a coup.

The king in the company of Richard was received with great acclaim in London, being greeted by the mayor, the two sheriffs and the aldermen dressed in scarlet, together with 500 horsemen. The *Great Chronicle* adds that the king was dressed in blue velvet, but the Duke of Gloucester and all the servants wore mourning of coarse black cloth.[8]

At the council meeting held on 10 May, Richard's protectorate was confirmed and, perhaps aware of the need for a show of stability and calm, the council agreed that the coronation should finally take place on 22 June. Richard arranged for mayor, aldermen and *"all the lords spiritual and temporal"* [9] to swear a public oath of fealty to the new king. It is difficult to believe, though it cannot be completely ruled out, that, in age when oaths were regarded as binding not only temporally, but spiritually, on the pain of serious offence before God, Richard, who had made a personal oath of loyalty himself in York and had another oath administered in London, should through an unlawful usurpation of the throne have contemplated the breaking of these oaths initiated by himself.

The Woodvilles had been keen to hasten the king's coronation so that Richard's protectorate might be brought to an end. However, the agreement of a new date for the coronation revived fears that the conclusion of Richard's protectorate might yet create further instability as different factions sought to gain control and influence over the boy king. Accordingly, the extension of Richard's protectorate, until such time as the king was deemed fit to govern for himself, was submitted to parliament, while Richard himself continued with detailed preparations for the coronation at which forty squires were to be made knights.

The Woodvilles now began suffer the consequences of failure, for, although parliament refused to allow a charge of treason against Rivers to proceed, both he and Dorset, together with others of the faction, were removed from office and effectively stripped of most of their power. Richard was generous in rewarding Buckingham who had stood by him so loyally and on 16 May he was granted the *"offices of chief justice and chamberlain in South and North Wales, constable of the castles of Carmarthen and Cardigan, etc. in Wales and the governance and supervision of all the king's subjects in South and North Wales and the Marches"* and *"the supervision and power of array of the king's subjects in the counties of Salop, Hereford, Dorset and Wiltshire"*. Also in May he was granted the offices of *"constable of the castle of Aberystwyth, and constable of other castles and towns there, and in Salop and Hereford; steward of royal castles, lordships, manors, etc. in South Wales, the Marches, Salop, and Hereford, constable, steward and receiver of the castle, manor and town of Monmouth, and other castles, etc. in South Wales, North Wales and the Marches, part of the Duchy of Lancaster, constable, steward and receiver of Usk, and of other castles, lordships, etc. in North Wales, South Wales, the Marches, Salop and Hereford, part of the earldom of March, justice and chamberlain of North Wales, constable and captain of the castle and town of Conway, and other castles in North Wales, etc."* [10]

Despite rewarding others who had offered their support, Richard was keen to demonstrate a continuity of administration rather than a rupture by retaining many of Edward's appointees in their positions and by appointing as chancellor the Bishop of Lincoln, John Russell, whose allegiance to Edward was well-known. And with Hastings remaining at the heart of the administration, it was hoped that the stability of the administration would help to ensure a trouble-free succession.

On his arrival in London, the young king had been lodged in the bishop's palace in St Paul's churchyard. However, since this was found to be inconvenient and insecure, parliament debated the best place for his residence, before finally agreeing with Hastings's suggestion of the Tower of London, which at that time was regarded as a royal residence, although parts of it had been used as a prison.[11] In fact, it possessed well-appointed royal apartments in which Edward took up residence.

It has been a matter of debate when Richard formulated his plan to take the throne. The anti-Richard view, which emphasises his hypocrisy and secret dealing, tends to suppose that he had already formed the plan by April 1483 and that, the protectorate being insufficient to satisfy his ambition, the seizing of Edward at Stony Stratford formed part of his scheme of usurpation.

On the other hand, if Richard had decided on this plan so early, there is still the problem of the oaths; and Edward's seizure could hardly have been part of long-considered scheme, for it relied more on the particular circumstances of the Woodville plan to hurry the king to London. Richard was also heavily involved in preparations for the coronation and was prepared to let parliament decide whether his protectorate should be extended. If we are take the view that Richard's loyalty to Edward and his military exploits point to a man headstrong and trustworthy, rather than one given to careful and subtle political deliberation, we might incline to the view that his plot to overthrow Edward was much more likely to have been conceived hurriedly. The seizure of Edward was an immediate expedient to ensure his protectorate, but the provisional nature of the security that this offered dawned on Richard only after the date for the coronation was set, when he realised that further action would be necessary. At his accession, Edward was twelve years of age, and, even supposing that Richard's protectorate had been extended, medieval monarchs had traditionally taken on the government of the realm from between the ages of about fourteen and sixteen, and so it would be perhaps only two years, at the most four, before Edward ruled in his own right. This would considerably weaken Richard's position, assuming that the young king, being kindly disposed towards Rivers with whom he had been brought up, resented his treatment by his uncle and sought to restore to power the Woodville faction, eager for revenge on Richard; furthermore, even at twelve, and although Richard was his protector, it would be difficult to remove him from the influence of his mother Elizabeth. The only way in which he could protect himself would be to become king himself.

However, there is a third, and more likely explanation, which involved the disturbing and momentous revelation of Bishop Stillington, a revelation whose impact was to have wide-reaching consequences. Although both Mancini and the Croyland chronicler refer to it, the evidence is provided by Commines alone and so may not be entirely trustworthy.[12]

Sometime at the beginning of June the Bishop of Bath and Wells, Robert Stillington revealed to Richard that his brother Edward had been pre-contracted to Eleanor Butler, thus making his marriage to Elizabeth Woodville invalid, their children illegitimate and Edward ineligible to succeed to the throne. As the sole witness to the pre-contract, and with Eleanor and more recently Edward having died, he was the only person surviving who knew of its existence. Immediate scepticism in the face of such a revelation, which overturned what had been understood and accepted, and changed the political landscape, was countered by the remembrance of Edward's womanising and by his secret marriage to Elizabeth, which seemed to invest the story with, at the least, the possibility of authenticity.

As any documentation recording the marriage has disappeared, much depends upon the reliability of Stillington. He was a Yorkist and his advancement is to some extent the result of this allegiance. If he had knowledge of the pre-contract it would provide an explanation for his receipt of a large annual salary in 1461, the year that the pre-contract was made and for his elevation to the see of Bath and Wells in 1465, the year of Edward's marriage to Elizabeth. Stillington, perhaps as a means to ensure his silence at a critical time, was arrested shortly after Clarence's execution in March 1478, only being released in June after being granted a pardon for the conveniently vague crime of speaking about things *"prejudicial to the King and his State"* and quite possibly under an injunction not to reveal what he knew. Those who see such a disclosure as a convenient fiction to legitimise Richard's accession, rather than the reason for his claim to the throne wonder why Stillington had not made his concerns known earlier. However, it is easy to understand why Stillington might have kept his silence during the reign of Edward; and after his death the Woodvilles were powerful enough to force him to refrain from speaking out. But once Richard, by taking charge of young Edward, had established his protectorate strongly enough to resist the Woodvilles, Stillington felt safe enough to reveal the truth that would prevent the sacrilege of an illegitimate child being crowned. It is probably not enough to claim that Richard could have allowed the accession, on the grounds that coronation would wipe out the fact of the illegitimacy, because there was no precedent for such a proceeding; and, in any case, the Yorkist cause would always be vulnerable if their king had such a stain on his birth.

Although there is no evidence that he received any favours from Richard, for instance he was not restored to his position as chancellor - and, in fact, in 1473 he had disputed Richard's claim to the lands of the Countess of Oxford - it is not impossible that the whole story was a fabrication concocted to give Richard's claim legitimacy.

There is a suspicion that, if the story were true, it could explain why Edward, who had previously forgiven Clarence for treacherous and disloyal behaviour had agreed to his execution, for, if Clarence had threatened to reveal what had perhaps had come to his ears regarding the pre-contract, there were dire consequences for Elizabeth, who saw that she stood lose everything she had gained for herself and her family, forcing her to pressure the king to have him silenced. Although there is no direct evidence that Stillington revealed anything to Clarence, his diocese extended into some of Clarence's land and, as we have seen he was arrested not long after Clarence was executed.

There is, however, an alternative hypothesis about how Richard came to know of the pre-contract between Eleanor Butler and Edward proposed by Peter Hancock, but to discuss this is to anticipate events, so we shall consider this a little later.

Richard called for forces to reinforce him in London from the City of York on 10 June and from Lord Neville of Raby on the day following. He claimed that the needed them *"ayanst the Quiene, hir blode adherents and affinitie, which have entended and daly doith intend to murder and utterly destroy"* him and Buckingham and *"and the old royall blode of this realme"*, going on to assert that their plot was by then widely known and encompassed in addition *"the finall distruccion and disheryson"* of *"thenheritours and men of honer, as weile of the north parties as odir contrees that belongen to us"*. It is an open question whether Richard genuinely feared another Woodville plot, or whether he was gathering strength for a plot of his own, though mention of a plot against the old royal blood hints at the Woodvilles. This calling for troops does not support the notion that Richard had pre-planned his actions at the council meeting in the Tower and his claim to the throne, because these reinforcements could never have arrived in time to provide help.

Richard next turned against some members of the council. Those familiar with Shakespeare's *Richard III* will have a strong impression of the scene where the wicked Richard breaks up the council meeting with denunciations of plots and sorcery against him and contrives the death of Hastings. The events themselves described by the chroniclers were indeed dramatic, though they differ in important respects from Shakespeare's biased portrayal, and have been the subject of much speculation about what they reveal concerning Richard's state of mind and motivation. One account states plainly that there was plot against Richard.[13]

> ...ther was dyvers imagenyd the deth of the duke of Gloceter, and hit was asspiyd and the Lord Hastings was takyn in the Towur and byhedyd forthwith, the xiij day of Iune Anno 1483. And the archbeschope of Yorke, the bischop of Ele and Oleuer King the secoudare, with other moo, was arestyd the same day and put in preson in the Towur.

Mancini and the *Croyland Chronicle* supply more details, cast doubt on the alleged plot and take a clear anti-Richard stance; yet, it is also unclear how far either of these can be relied upon to give a fair and accurate record of the events of 13 June.

Mancini wrote that even with power of the royal blood in his hand, Richard felt that he had to remove or imprison those who had been the closest friends of Edward IV and who might be expected to be loyal to his son, especially Hastings, Morton, the Bishop of Ely, and Rotherham, the Archbishop of York, whom Richard had already removed from the office of chancellor. Richard had learned from Buckingham that they sometimes met in each other's houses. On the day of the council meeting in the Tower, Richard, as pre-arranged, cried out that an ambush had been prepared for him and that traitors had come with hidden arms. Soldiers rushed in with Buckingham and cut down Hastings on the pretext of treason, and arrested the archbishop and the bishop, who were spared by virtue of being in holy orders. The townsmen, hearing the uproar, panicked and seized weapons, but Richard dispatched a herald to calm the situation by proclaiming that, although there had been a plot, the originator, Hastings, had paid the penalty. *"At first the ignorant crowd believed, although the real truth was on the lips of many, namely that the plot had been feigned by the duke so as to escape the odium of such a crime."*[14]

However, the Croyland chronicler tells a somewhat different story.[15]

> *For, the day previously, the Protector had, with singular adroitness, divided the council, so that one part met in the morning at Westminster, and the other at the Tower of London, where the king was. The lord Hastings, on the thirteenth day of the month of June, being the sixth day of the week, on coming to the Tower to join the council, was, by order of the Protector, beheaded. Two distinguished prelates, also, Thomas, archbishop of York, and John, bishop of Ely, out of respect for their order, held exempt from capital punishment, were carried prisoners to different castles in Wales.*

The *Great Chronicle's* account is more in agreement with the *Croyland Chronicle* than with Mancini.[16]

> *And upon the same day Lord Hastings dined with him and, after dinner, rode behind him or behind the Duke of Buckingham to the Tower, where, when they with the other lords had entered the council*

> chamber and had communed for a while of such matters as he had previously proposed, suddenly one made an outcry at the council chamber door, "Treason! Treason!", and forthwith the usher opened the door and then pressed in such men as were before appointed and straightway laid hands upon the Earl of Derby and the Lord Hastings; and at once, without any process of law or lawful examination, led Lord Hastings out unto the green beside the chapel and there, upon an end of a squared piece of timber, without any long confession or other space of remembrance, struck off his head. ...And in like manner would the earl of Derby have been dealt with, as the fame went, saving [that the protector] feared the Lord Strange, the earl's son, who was then in Lancashire, wherefore he was immediately set at liberty without hurt, except that his face was grazed a little with some weapon when the tyrants first entered the chamber. Then were the Archbishop of York, Doctor Rotherham, and the Bishop Ely, Doctor Morton, set in surety for a time...

The detail about Stanley, the Earl of Derby is an interesting one. At first it seems to suggest a measure of cowardice on Richard's part, being unwilling, through fear, to carry out his initial purpose. But more likely it provides contradictory evidence for the assertion that the meeting, arrests and execution were carefully pre-planned by Richard, for if everything had been so carefully planned beforehand then, knowing the position of Stanley, he would never have arrested him in the first place. The scene suggests a high degree of improvisation and then it is not impossible to discount the supposition that whoever had cried *"Treason"* had discovered good cause for his fears, especially if, as Richard alleged, there was a plot.

Sir Thomas More provides an entertaining account, perhaps indeed aimed more at arousing interest than in conveying the strict truth.[17] According to More, when Richard came into the council meeting he was courteous and, after apologising for his lateness and some *"little talking"*, requested that the Bishop of Ely, Morton, send for some strawberries from his garden. Richard then left the meeting for about an hour, but when he returned his countenance was changed to one of anger. He frowned, knitted his brows, and gnawed his lips. Sitting down he asked what should be the reward of those who plotted his death. The lords wondered whom Richard had in mind, because they all thought themselves innocent. Hastings, however, supported by the others, replied that they deserved to be punished as traitors. Richard then accused Elizabeth Woodville and Jane Shore, now Hastings' mistress, of witchcraft, in proof of which he showed them his withered arm, which in fact had always been withered. Hastings was relieved by this charge, because it was levelled against the queen rather than someone he *"loved better"*. When Hastings answered that if it were it were *"heinously done"* and they deserved *"heinous punishment"*, Richard flew into a rage protesting that Hastings served him with *"ifs and ands"* and called him a traitor. He then rapped on the table and someone outside the chamber cried, *"Treason!"* at which armed men poured in. Hastings was arrested, allowed a short confession and was executed shortly thereafter on a log on the green beside the chapel, because Richard wanted to make haste for his dinner.

Morton, no friend to Richard, a Lancastrian sympathiser, though supporting the House of York when expedient, always a trimmer, and partisan of the Woodville cause, on whose memories More may have based his narrative, may be accounted an unreliable witness. Indeed, if he had himself been guilty of treachery, his reluctance to admit it and to manufacture a version favourable to himself is understandable. If we may question the veracity of the account of Richard referring to a withered arm, since neither of Richard's arms suffered from that deformity, so we may consider Richard's asking for strawberries as an invented detail designed to confer credibility. More, a man closely allied with the Tudors - at least before his split with Henry VIII -, had a clear interest in blackening Richard's character. It has even been questioned whether More intended to write a true history at all, rather than attempting a moral fable with a political dimension.

The truth is hard to discover. Certainly it appears that Morton, Hastings, Rotherham and Stanley had been planning something. Morton, as a strong supporter of Woodvilles, could well have instigated a plot, supported by Rotherham. The most interesting question is why Richard accused Hastings of treason. There are several possible explanations. One possibility is that although Hastings had given Richard military aid and supported him against the Woodvilles - Hastings' aim being merely to prevent the Woodvilles from gaining control of Edward V - he was appalled when he learned of Richard's plans to usurp the throne and acted accordingly. Another possibility is that he had changed sides to support the Woodvilles, being disappointed with his rewards for his assistance to Richard, especially when saw how well Buckingham had been rewarded. A further possibility is that Hastings, who had his own men London, had begun to pose an unexpected threat to Richard, who had to act immediately and not wait for the reinforcements which he had requested just three days previously. More claims that Catesby, an intimate of Hastings, had exposed Hastings' *"terrible woordes"* to Richard, but fails to specify exactly what Hastings was planning, whether it were: opposition to Richard's bid for power; his removal from power; his imprisonment; or his death. If Richard executed Hastings as a warning to others, his subsequent actions appear very strange, for he gave Hastings an honourable burial in St George's Chapel Windsor, removed the block that Hastings' treason had placed on his children's rights and allowed his widow to receive his estates. Of course, it is always possible that Richard, although possessing no hard evidence, had some reason to fear Hastings and decided to pre-empt any possible problem by acting first. It is the same dilemma that affects all rulers, states and individuals, in every age. How far can pre-emptive action against a perceived enemy, who it is possible might pose a serious threat against the state, be justified? Shakespeare considered the dilemma in *Julius Caesar*:[18]

> *And since the quarrel*
> *Will bear no colour for the thing he is,*
> *Fashion it thus: that what he is, augmented,*
> *Would run to these and these extremities.*
> *And therefore think him as a serpent's egg —*

Which, hatched, would as his kind grow mischievous—
And kill him in the shell.

We can now consider the theory proposed by Peter Hancock.[19] He contends that it was Catesby who first informed Richard about the pre-contract, Bishop Stillington providing only confirmation. There had been significant contact, especially concerning legal affairs, between Eleanor Butler's family and the Catesbys, in particular with William Catesby's father Sir William, who was a lawyer. It was this connection that led to Catesby's knowledge of the pre-contract. Hastings was also aware of the pre-contract and when Catesby intimated to Richard that he had important information on the morning of the Council meeting in the Tower, Richard called for an adjournment while he considered the situation and his response to it. Loyalty being of prime importance to him, he felt especially betrayed by Hastings who had kept this knowledge from him, knowledge that gave him a legitimate claim to the throne, and for this reason ordered his summary execution. Once Richard was in possession of this knowledge, Stillington was merely required to testify as to its truth. Catesby's role provides an explanation as to why he was handsomely rewarded by Richard, becoming perhaps the second most powerful man in the land. However, an objection to this theory remains. If Hastings had been executed for disloyalty in failing to reveal his knowledge, surely Catesby, though not bound to Richard by the same ties of friendship, would not have escaped punishment simply by virtue of being the first to break silence.

In executing Hastings, Richard had acted in a characteristically impulsive manner, more concerned to counter the dangers of an immediate threat than to consider the wider political consequences. While action against the unpopular Woodvilles was more likely to gain popular approval than otherwise, the execution of Hastings, who commanded a strong following was a different matter, not only because summary execution brought into question Richard's motives, but also because Hastings had provided important political and military support, without which Richard was weakened. Perhaps it was a recognition of how weak his position had become that convinced Richard that the only way in which he could command sufficient power to guarantee his own security was to take the throne himself. However, even that may give an overly cynical view of the motives of a man, who, if the report of Edward's pre-contract was correct, had an entirely legitimate claim to the crown.

With the main threat seemingly removed, Richard restored Stanley to the council and released Rotherham, keeping only the dangerous Morton imprisoned in Buckingham's charge. Jane Shore was arrested for her part in the plot, being the means by which Hastings communicated with Elizabeth. The Bishop of London found her guilty of being a harlot and sentenced her to walk the public streets barefoot, carrying a lit taper in front of a cross and singing psalms. More says that she went with *"countenance and pace demure"* and *"so fair and louely"* that she won great praise. She was then imprisoned at Ludgate. However, Richard did not bear a grudge against her, for, after his solicitor Thomas Lynom petitioned to marry her, he gave his consent to the match, if Bishop Russell failed to convince him of his foolishness, though he commented that in being willing to marry her he must be *"marvellously blinded and abused"*.

The Croyland chronicler writes that on the Monday following Hastings's execution Richard and Buckingham *"came with a great multitude by water to Westminster, armed with swords and staves, and compelled the cardinal lord archbishop of Canterbury, with many others, to enter the sanctuary, in order to appeal to the good feelings of the queen and prompt her to allow her son, Richard, duke of York, to come forth and proceed to the Tower, that he might comfort the king his brother. In words, assenting with many thanks to this proposal, she accordingly sent the boy, who was conducted by the lord cardinal to the king in the Tower of London"*.[20]

Mancini expressed the view that Elizabeth released the boy through fear of the armed men surrounding the sanctuary and because she believed the archbishop when he said that the boy would be restored to her after his brother's coronation.[21] The writer of the *Great Chronicle* attributes cowardice and duplicity to the Richard writing that he *"behaved so gloriously unto the queen with his manifold dissimulated fair promises that neither she nor yet the archbishop had in them any manner of suspicion of guile".*[22] Yet, if Hastings had already been executed under a false charge of treason, surely the queen, not known for submitting quietly, though aware that the council might yet decide to support Buckingham in his argument that a child could not seek sanctuary, would have been mindful of any danger in releasing her son to Richard. If indeed she suspected Richard's motives, it is surprising that she did not force Richard's hand to seize the boy with violence, securing at least a moral victory and damage to Richard's prestige, if the boy's claim to sanctuary was finally upheld. Although More and Polydore Vergil place the removal of Richard from sanctuary before Hastings' execution, in order to suggest that Elizabeth did not know of Richard's ruthlessness, it would seem that this event took place after the execution.

The Princes in the Tower

There is also the question of why Richard needed the boy under his control, for if the charges of illegitimacy were true, and Richard was already aware of them, both boys would have been disbarred from the throne. It is unlikely that Richard, despite his own troubled childhood, was prompted by compassion for the lonely brother in the Tower, as he went to the trouble of taking a large force of soldiers to Westminster, seemingly to force the issue. The truth is probably that Richard recognised that any offspring of Edward under the control of the Woodvilles might provide a focus for discontent and rebellion, legitimate or not; after all, he had seen sufficient evidence during the course of his own life that what was sanctioned by the law could be overturned by those wielding the greater might, under the pretence of a mere show of legitimacy, which action would be generally accepted either through fear or through negligence in failing to perceive the pretence.

On Sunday, 22 June 1483, Dr Ralph Shaw (or Shaa or Sha) preached a sermon attended by many lords spiritual and temporal, including Buckingham, at St Paul's Cross, which was traditionally used for political speeches. Richard himself apparently made a late appearance. The text taken by Shaw was Wisdom 4:3 *"Spuria vitulamina non agent radices altas"* – *"Bastard slips shall not take deep root"*. In this sermon he explained how the invalid marriage between Edward IV and Elizabeth Woodville had made both their sons illegitimate and hence disqualified from them claiming the throne; and that, accordingly, Richard was the rightful king, since Clarence's attainder had ruled out his son, Edward, Earl of Warwick. There was cruel irony for Edward in that this sermon was preached on the very day that his mother had planned to have him crowned as Edward V. But this sermon, like so much else concerning Richard, is surrounded by confusion. The text no longer survives and, since reports of its contents differ, the truth is hard to discern. Thomas More wrote that the sermon went further than proclaiming the illegitimacy of Edward's offspring and that it made the shocking assertion that *"neither King Edward himself nor the Duke of Clarence were lawfully begotten, nor were the very children of the Duke of Yorke, but gotten vnlawfully by other parsons by thaduoutry of the duchess their mother"*.[23] If this was true, it was a repetition of the rumour that had been current in some circles for a number of years. However, as so often with More, significant errors, either deliberate or intended continually intrude, for he also stated that *"Dame Elisabeth Lucy was verily the wife of king Edward, and so the prince and all his children bastardes that were gotten vpon the quene"*.[24] Here, the identification of Elisabeth Lucy as Edward's partner in the pre-contract instead of Eleanor Butler, might be a fault of memory, or, as has been suggested, an attempt to cover up the truth. Thus, it is hard to place confidence in More's other assertions. Vergil, however, agreed with More that the sermon did reveal Edward IV's illegitimacy.[25]

> *Sha…began to instruct the people by many reasons, how that the late king Edward was not begotten by Richard duke of York, but by some other, who pryvyly and by stelth had had knowledge of his mother; and that the same did manifestly appeare by sure demonstrations, because king Edward was nether in physonomy nor shape of body lyke unto Richard the father; for he was highe of stature, thither very little; he of large face, thither short and rownd.*

He offers, as proof of this, the reaction of Cecily, Richard's mother.

> *…Cecyly, king Edwards mother, as ys before sayd, being falsely accussyd of adultery, complaynd afterward in sundry places to right many noble men, wherof some yeat lyve, of that great injury which hir soon Richard had doon her.*

The outrage affected by some chroniclers and earlier historians at the content of the sermon, having little to do with a genuine indignation, unless it were an indignation at the revelation of such embarrassing details to the common folk, was rather a rhetorical weapon to employ against Richard. Vergil reports:

> *Whan the people herd hese words, they wer wooderus vehemently trublyd in mind therwith, as men who, abassyd with the shamefulness of the matter, all to be cursyd and detestyd as well the rashnes,*

> *foolehardyness, and doltishnes of the preacher as the madness of Richard the duks wycked mynde, who wold not se how great shame yt was to his owne howse and to the whole realme, how great dishonour and blot, to condemne, in open audience, his mother of adultery, a woman of most pure and honourable life; to imprint upon his excellent and good brother the note of perpetuall infamy; to lay upon his most innocent nephewes and everlasting reproche. Wherfor at the very instant yow might have sene some astoyned with the noveltie and strangenes of the thing, stand a mad man in a mase; others all agast with thowtrageous crueltie of thorrible fact, to be in gteat feare of themselves because they war frindes of the chyldre, whom they adjudgyd now utterly undone...*

Vergil's attempt to manipulate his readers is obvious. In the context of adultery and illegitimacy, nobody could seriously claim that the notoriously womanising and dissolute Edward was an *"excellent and good brother"*, unless to discredit Richard. Moreover, Vergil seems more concerned that the affair was aired to *"an open audience"* than he is with disproving the charge, and his description of people's responses does not read true, since such revelations, then as now, would be far more likely to evoke prurient interest and enthusiastic gossip than the reactions he is at pains to describe.

A typical reaction is that of David Hume writing in the eighteenth century, who makes little attempt to refute the allegation merely indicating his disapproval of Richard for supporting it.

> *Nothing can be imagined more impudent than this assertion, which threw so foul an imputation on his own mother, a princess of irreproachable virtue...*

The rejoinder to this is that if the allegation were indeed true, it would be, to say the least, an impudence of the highest order to have passed off an illegitimate child as the true heir to the throne; and, as shown earlier, there are good grounds for believing that Edward IV was illegitimate.

Mancini expressed no doubts as to what he imagined Richard's intentions to be. He describes him as, putting aside the mourning clothes that he had been wearing since Edward's death and, dressing himself in purple to ride publicly through the capital surrounded by a thousand attendants. Aiming to receive the attention and applause as protector, he secretly entertained in his private dwellings an increasingly large number of men. Mancini's implication is that he was plotting to usurp the throne and that everybody understood what his real aims were.[26]

Buckingham repeated the claim of the illegitimacy of Edward's sons in a speech on 24 June in the Guildhall. However, if sources such as the *Great Chronicle of London*, Vergil and More are to be given credence, people in general were grievously troubled by these claims and gave them less than whole-hearted support, despite the reported skill and eloquence of Buckingham. More, for instance recounts that at the end of Buckingham's speech the audience, instead of crying for King Richard, was *"husht and mute"* and finally the only response was a feeble *"kynge Richarde, kynge Richarde"* from some placemen thrust into the back of the hall. Yet, as we have already learnt, it is unwise to place too much trust in the details presented by these sources and the interpretations of their authors. If there had been so much distrust of Richard, it is difficult to see why parliament should give him such overwhelming support and if one were minded to show how discredited he was in the eyes of people generally, it would be easy to record falsely a lack of public acclamation.

The legitimacy of the parliament held on 25 June which declared Richard to have the true title to the throne has been questioned on two grounds. Firstly a writ of *supersedeas* was received at York ordering that representatives should not to be sent; and secondly the summons was issued in the name of the deceased Edward IV. Therefore, so it is argued, the throne lay vacant with no claimant, since Clarence's son was attainted and the Prince Edward declared illegitimate; it followed there was no king officially to open parliament, because Richard, who was next in succession, had made no formal claim. However, Prince Edward had not yet been formally declared illegitimate, though it was this assembly that would do so, for it seems that it was during this assembly that the illegitimacy of all Edward's children was declared, through his invalid marriage to Elizabeth, and Richard's right to succeed established. Yet again, as with so many things to do with Richard, the exact truth is difficult to ascertain.

The next day, the Duke of Buckingham headed a delegation to Baynard's Castle to present the petition to Richard, who proceeded to Westminster Hall where he symbolically took his place on the marble chair of King's Bench flanked by the Dukes of Norfolk and Suffolk. He made a formal claim to the crown having given a speech to win people to his cause and proclaimed a pardon for all who had opposed him, in token of which he had a certain Fogge brought out of sanctuary and took him by the hand as a sign of his pardon.[27] Thus his reign began.

The original petition to Richard has not survived, although the *Titulus Regius* passed by parliament on 23rd January 1484 claims to be based on this petition, and there is no reason to doubt this.

> ...be it ordained, provided and established in this present Parliament, that the tenor of the said Roll, with all the continue of the same, presented, as is above said, and delivered to our before said Sovereign Lord the King...

In fact, one of the aims of the *Titulus Regius* was to remove any doubt about the legality of the previous petition and to give no grounds for any doubt about Richard's right to succeed. It is a quirk of history that Richard had a more strongly founded parliamentary title to the crown than any other king of the Middle Ages. It was perhaps to be expected that Richard, though wishing to maintain administrative continuity with his brother's rule, should wish to denounce the invalid marriage to Elizabeth and to denigrate some of the more notorious features of that time, especially the Woodville influence.

> Over this, amongst other things, more specially we consider how that, the time of the Reign of King Edward IV, late deceased, after the

ungracious pretensed marriage, as all England had cause so to say, made between the said King Edward IV and Elizabeth, sometime wife to Sir John Grey, Knight, late naming herself and many years heretofore Queen of England, the order of all politic rule was perverted, the laws of God and of God's Church, and also the laws of nature, and of England, and also the laudable customs and liberties of the same, wherein every Englishman is inheritor; broken, subverted and contempted, against all reason and justice, so that this Land was ruled by self-will and pleasure, fear and dread, all manner of equity and laws laid apart and despised, whereof ensued many inconveniences and mischiefs, as murders, extortions and oppressions, namely of poor and impotent people, so that no man was sure of his life, land nor livelihood, nor of his wife, daughter nor servant, every good maiden and woman standing in dread to be ravished and defouled. And besides this, what discords, inward battles, effusion of Christian men's blood and namely, by the destruction of the noble blood of this Land, was had and committed within the same, it is evident and notary [notorious] through all this Realm unto the great sorrow and heaviness of all true Englishmen.

And here also we consider how that the said pretensed marriage was made privately and secretly, with edition of banns, in a private chamber, a profane place, and not openly in the face of the church, after the laws of God's church, but contrary thereunto, and the laudable custom of the Church of England. And how also, that at the time of the contract of the same pretensed marriage, and before and long time after, the said King Edward was and stood married and troth plight to one Dame Eleanor Butler, daughter of the old Earl of Shrewsbury, with whom the said King Edward had made a precontract of matrimony, long time before he made the said pretensed marriage with the said Elizabeth Grey [Woodville] in manner and form aforesaid. Which premises being true, as in very truth they been true, it appears and follows evidently, that the said King Edward during his life, and the said Elizabeth, lived together sinfully and damnably in adultery, against the law of God and his Church; and

> *therefore no marvel that the sovereign Lord and head of this Land, being of such ungodly disposition, and provoking the ire and indignation of our Lord God, such heinous mischiefs and inconveniences, as is above remembered, were used and committed in the Realm amongst the subjects. Also it appears evidently and follows that all the issue and children of the said King, been [being] bastards, and unable to inherit or to claim anything by inheritance, by the law and custom of England.*

However, though the tone is exaggerated, the act certainly appears to show that there was at least much disquiet over the way Edward ruled, that the country was not well-contented and that he was not an *"excellent and good brother"*, a description Vergil used to provide a contrast with his portrayal of Richard.

The act also confirmed Richard's title.

> *Over this we consider, how that you be the undoubted son and heir of Richard late Duke of York, very inheritor to the said crown and dignity royal and as in right King of England, by way to inheritance, and that at this time the premises duly considered, there is none other person living but you only, that by right may claim the said crown and dignity royal, by way of inheritance, and how that you be born within this Land; by reason whereof, as we deem in our minds, you be more naturally inclined to the prosperity and common weal of the same: and all the three Estates of the Land have, and may have, more certain knowledge of your birth and affiliation above said. We consider also, the great wit, prudence, justice, princely courage, and the memorable and laudable acts in diverse battles, which as we by experience know you heretofore have done for the salvation and defence of this same Realm; and also the great nobility and excellence of your birth and blood, as of him that is descended of the three most royal houses in Christendom, that is to say, England, France and Spain.*

It is by chance that the act has come down to us, for in a typically calculating and cynical fashion, reminiscent of more recent totalitarian regimes, Henry VII not only had this act repealed, but ordered all copies of it to be destroyed. This was not his only attempt to rewrite history to try to provide legitimacy and stability for his rule, for in a peculiarly nasty and vindictive piece of legislation he had the beginning of his reign dated the day before the Battle of Bosworth, so making all those who had legitimately fought for the true king, Richard, traitors. Fortunately a copy did survive the otherwise meticulously ruthless Henry and was discovered in the Tower of London.

No doubt pragmatism also featured in the acceptance of Richard's succession. Even if some people harboured doubts over his attaining crown, he was a member of the royal house, he had a stable powerbase that would help to secure his administration, the uncertain rule of a minor under the Woodville influence would be avoided and, perhaps most importantly, in a land exhausted by previous conflicts, his rule might prevent civil war from breaking out once more.

On 6 July 1483 Richard was crowned in Westminster Abbey in a ceremony attended with much pomp. The expensive fabrics ordered for Edward's coronation were conveniently at hand. The barefoot king and queen following the heralds and trumpeters walked in procession to Westminster Abbey. The Archbishop of Canterbury and other bishops preceded the nobility. At the high altar the King and Queen were anointed with the chrism (the holy oil), and having been dressed in robes of cloth of gold were crowned. Almost all of the nobility was present, including Margaret Beaufort, mother of the future King Henry VII, who carried Anne's train. After his coronation Richard left the beautifully crafted vial which had contained the holy oil of chrism in the safe keeping of the Abbey of Westminster. A detailed account of the coronation and its attendant ceremonies can found in the Appendix.

It is not possible to assert that the attendance of the lords spiritual and temporal as well as other men of influence argues the universal popularity of Richard. Clearly he did have many strong supporters, but there must have been some, schooled in those turbulent times, who calculated that making a show of supporting the current king was the most reasonable course, while at the same time keeping a close watch for when the time might dictate a change of allegiance. Others might have hidden their hostility to Richard under the pretence of loyalty, perjuring themselves in swearing the oath of loyalty. Besides, since many of the nobility had presented themselves in London for Edward's coronation, it would be a too obvious and reckless a snub to fail to attend Richard's.

Among his true supporters Richard could count on William Dudley, Bishop of Durham; Robert Stillington, Bishop of Bath and Wells; John Russell, Bishop of Lincoln; Thomas Langton, Bishop of St David's; and the Dukes of Buckingham and Norfolk. In addition, he could count on a number of other nobles, his supporters from the north and the Knights of the Bath he had just created. Many of these men had benefited from Richard's patronage.

-6-

King Richard

The Tudor chroniclers, and some other historians, assumed from the smooth success of Richard's ascent to the throne, which was achieved with remarkably little bloodshed, that it was the result of a carefully conceived plan, disloyal from its inception and devious in its execution. Yet, as when considering Bismarck's successful reunification of Germany in the nineteenth century, it can be a mistake to conclude that because a difficult objective has been achieved it must have been the result of meticulous calculation. We should be on safer ground when considering the ascent of Richard - a man with more interest in military action than politics, more headstrong, or decisive than calculating, a man who in an insecure age craved security - to see him at each stage acting to preserve his immediate interest, but also led by his own pre-emptive actions and by the course of events to the point where succeeding to the throne became a logical, political and, if Edward's children truly were illegitimate, moral necessity.

On the same day as the parliamentary assembly met, 25 June, Rivers, Vaughan and Grey were executed on a charge of treason at Pontefract Castle and, most historians assume, without the benefit of a trial, though it is certainly possible that Percy did preside over a court. Such summary executions, however, while part of the unpleasant political realities of the age, would undermine the principles of justice and respect for the processes of law that Richard aimed to establish and place an ugly stain on his reputation. Yet the more pertinent question is whether or not the three were guilty of the treason for which they were executed. This is difficult to determine. They did, however, co-operate with Elizabeth in attempting to whisk Edward to his coronation, which was, as we have seen, an attempt to frustrate Edward IV's will by bringing to an end Richard's protectorate and to consolidate Woodville power. Although Richard was not king, plotting against the protectorate could be considered treason, since it was a rebellion against the government of the realm. Two days before his execution, and, therefore, almost certainly in anticipation of it, Rivers made Richard supervisor of his will. This was not the first time that Rivers had shown trust in Richard's judgement and sense of fairness, for in March 1483 he had submitted an important property case to him. If he had been guiltless it is difficult to understand why he would have placed so much trust in a king who demanded his execution.

Despite the criticisms of Edward's reign made in the *Titulus Regius*, Richard, in the knowledge that he was regarded by the southern lords with some suspicion, aimed to emphasise the continuity of Yorkist rule. Thus he did little to alter the *status quo*, although Buckingham was rewarded with posts of Chief Justice and Chamberlain in north and south Wales, Constable and Steward of the king's castles in Shropshire and Hereford and with the position of Great Chamberlain. Percy was given the wardenship of the West March and Richard's palatinate in Cumberland. John Howard was made Duke of Norfolk, Marshal of England and Admiral of England, and received a sizeable portion of crown lands. In addition, Viscount Lovell was created Lord Chamberlain of the household, following Hastings' execution, William Catesby was made Chancellor of the Exchequer and Chancellor of the Earldom of March, Thomas Metcalfe became Chancellor of the Duchy of Lancaster, and John Kendall was appointed Richard's secretary.

The men led by Sir Richard Ratcliffe, who had been summoned by Richard for his own protection had arrived in London in time for the coronation, and were mocked for their rusty armour. The *Chronicle of London* puts their number at about four or five thousand, which is most likely an exaggeration. Even after Richard dismissed them, some remained in the south to cause trouble and had to be disciplined by Richard himself *"who put some in execution and so pacified the country"*.

Richard recognised that his power-base was relatively weak and sought to rectify this by embarking on a glorious royal progress. Among those accompanying him were some of the most powerful lords spiritual and temporal. Richard was careful to include the calculating and untrustworthy Stanley, so as to avoid the possibility of him fomenting trouble in his absence. The progress took a route via Windsor and Reading to Oxford where Richard attended debates on moral philosophy and theology. At Woodstock he made the popular decision to reverse Edwards IV's annexation of the Forest of Wychwood and to return the land to the people, since this annexation was *"against conscience and to the public damage"*. While in Gloucester he granted the city a charter of liberties, and proceeding to Tewkesbury, made a generous (perhaps politic) donation of £300 to the Abbey, where Clarence and Henry VI's son were buried. According to Rous, at Worcester he declined an offer of money from the people as he had done before in London and Gloucester *"affirming that he would rather have their love than their treasure"*. Of course, it is easy to be cynical about Richard's motives, but for those who are the whipping boys of history almost any good work can be dismissed as an example of hypocrisy or as a concealment of ulterior motives. The Bishop of St David's, Thomas Langton, who was one of the party, was less suspicious and, seeing the good in Richard wrote (as we have already seen):

> *I trust to God soon, by Michaelmas, the king shall be in London. He contents the people wherever he goes better than ever did any prince; for many a poor man that has suffered wrong many days has been relieved and helped by him and his commands in his progress. And in many great cities and towns were great sums of money which were given to him which he has refused. On my faith I never liked the qualities of a prince as well as his. God has sent him to us for the welfare of us all.*

It seems that it was at Nottingham that Edward, Richard's son was invested as Prince of Wales.[1]

> ...*we have made and created, and do make and create, him Prince of Wales and Earl of Chester. And have given and granted and do give and grant to the same Edward the name style title dignity and honour of the said principality and earldom...And we invest him as the custom is by the girding on of the sword, the handing over and setting of the garland on his head, and of the gold ring on his finger, and of the gold staff in his hand, to have and to hold to him and his heirs, kings of England, for ever.*

Richard's visit to York was a great triumph, accompanied with grand ceremonies. The streets of the city were decked with tapestries and cloth of arras, and on 29 August Richard was formally greeted outside the city walls by the mayor and other leading citizens dressed in robes of scarlet and red. The *Bedern College Statute Book* has a detailed record of the event.[2]

> *After being received by the authorities in solemn procession at the chapel of St James outside the walls, they were honourably received into the City, and passed through displays and decorations to the Metropolitan Church of St Peter. Here the King was honourably received at the west door by the Dean and Canons and other ministers, all vested in blue silk copes, sprinkled with holy water and censed. On an ornamental footstool at the font he said a Paternoster, the Succentor of the Vicars saying the responses to the De Trinitate, that is "Honor virtus", this being finished by the Choir before the steps of the High Altar. Here a pause was made for about a space of a Paternoster and an Ave. The Dean then began the prayer "Et ne nos inducas" for the King. This being done the Dean and Canons then withdrew into their stalls with other ministers and Amen finished on the organ. The psalm Te Deum followed, begun by the officiating prelate, and finished by the choir and the organ, at once the antiphon*

De Trintate was sung by the Succentor, that is "Gratias tibi Deus", with a versicle and a prayer to the Trinity. The procession then went to the palace of the Lord Archbishop.

On the feast of the Nativity of the Blessed Virgin Mary [8 September], the King and Queen both crowned went in procession to the aforesaid church, the Prince and all the other Lords, both spiritual and temporal being in attendance. The Bishop of Durham was the officiating prelate, and the High altar was ornamented with silver and gilt figures of the twelve Apostles and many other relics given by the Lord King. These remained there until the sixth hour. After Mass they all returned to the Palace and there before dinner, he [Edward] was created Prince by the Lord King, in the presence of all. And so they sat, crowned, for four hours, there being present the Dean, Robert Both, the Canons, that is Treasurer Portyngton, Archdeacon Potman of York and the Sub-Dean, and four other prebendaries, ten parsons and twelve Vicars with other ministers of the church.

The *Croyland Chronicle* also reports these events but not without a cynical comment, as though Richard could do nothing without it being part of some underhand scheme.[3]

Here [at York] on the day appointed for repeating his coronation in the metropolitan church, he also presented his only son, Edward, on whom the same day he had elevated to the rank of Prince of Wales with the insignia of the golden wand and the wreath upon his head; while at the same time, he gave most gorgeous and sumptuous feasts and banquets for the purpose of gaining the affections of the people. Nor were treasures by any means wanting, with which to satisfy the desires of his haughty mind; since he had taken possession of all those which the most glorious king Edward, his deceased brother, had, by dint of the greatest care and scrupulousness, amassed, as already stated, many years before, and had entrusted to the disposal of his executors as a means whereby to carry out the dispositions of his last will: all these he had seized, the very moment that he had contemplated the usurpation of the throne.

It is also worth noting that the *Chronicle* has it that the ceremony in York was a second coronation, as though Richard's pride was greedily unsatisfied with the first one. There is no other evidence for it being a second coronation, although it probably did provide the citizens of York with the opportunity to reaffirm their allegiance to Richard.

Polydore Vergil gives another account.[4]

In which procession very solemnly set furth and clebratyd by the clergy, the king was present in parson, adornyed with a notable riche dyademe, and accompanied with a great number of noble men: the queen folowyd also with a crowne upon hir head, who led by the hand hir soon Edward crownyd also with so great honour, joy, and congratulation of thinhabytants, as in shew of rejoysing they extollyd king Richard above the skyes.

It might at first seem strange that Vergil should describe the enthusiasm with which Richard was acclaimed, but Vergil was writing at the behest of Henry VII and his audience was mainly those powerful men in the south, who, despising the north and its lords, would take the northerners' support of Richard as further evidence of his unsuitability.

These three accounts give a good indication of the unreliability of the records regarding Richard. The Croyland chronicler states that there was a repetition of the coronation ceremony, but this is lacking in the record of the *Bedern College Statute Book,* and some chronicles assume that Edward was created Prince of Wales in York, though, as we have seen, the Harleian MS places this event in Nottingham. Whereas a restaging of both ceremonies at York for his loyal northern subjects cannot be ruled out entirely, a second coronation under these circumstances - bearing in mind that anointing a king was akin to the anointing at priestly ordinations, conferring an indelible authority - would be most unlikely; and Nottingham seems to have been the most likely venue for the Prince of Wales's investiture.

The charge that has lain most heavily on Richard's reputation is that he murdered his two nephews, the so-called Princes in the Tower.

Thomas More wrote that Richard conceived the plan of murdering the princes while on the royal progress, riding towards Gloucester, and sent John Green to Sir Robert Brackenbury, the constable of the Tower, *"with a letter and credence also, that the same sir Robert shoulde in any wise put the two children to death"*.[5] Brakenbury's conscience did not permit him to be responsible for such an act, and on his refusal Richard sent James Tyrell to organise their deaths, which he did, employing Miles Forest and John Dighton. When Tyrell came to see the bodies he ordered that they be buried *"at the starye foote, metely depe in the grounde vnder a great heape of stones"*.[6] But a priest of Brackenbury exhumed the bodies and reburied them in a secret place.

However, More is relying on the rumours circulating at the time and on a supposed (and most convenient) confession by Tyrell in the reign of Henry VII that no one else makes reference to. This confession has never been found, probably because it was an invention of More. Vergil, who would have had good reason to mention a confession, and who provides a broadly similar account, makes no mention of one.[7]

> *Thus Richard, without assent of the commaltie, by might and will of certane noblemen of his faction, enjoyed the realme, contrary to the law of God and man; who not long after, having establyshyd all thinges at London according to his owne fantasy, tooke his journey to York, and first he went streight to Glocester, where the whyle he taryed the haynous guylt of wicked conscyence dyd so freat him every moment as that he lyvyd in contynuall feare, for thexpelling wherof by any kind of meane he determynyd by death to dispatche his nephewys, because so long as they lyvyd he could never be out of hazard; wherefore he sent warrant to Robert Brakenbury, lyvetenant of the towr of London to procure ther death with all diligence, by some meane covenyent...But the lyvetenant of the towr of London after he had receavyd the kinges horryble commyssion was astonyd with the*

creweltie of the fact, and fearing least yf he showld obey the same might at one time or other turne to his owne hame, dyd therfor dyffer the dooing therof in hope that the kinge wold spare his owne bloode, or ther tender age, or alter that heavy determynation. But any one of those poynts was so fur from taking place, seing that the mynd therin remanyd immovable, as that when king Richard understoode the lyvetenant to make delay of that which he commandyd, hee anon commyttyd the charge of hastening that slawghter unto another, that is to say James Tyrell, who, being forcyd to do the kings commandment, rode sorowfully to London, and, to the woorst example that hath been almost ever hard [heard] of, murderyd those babes of thyssew [the issue] royal. Thys end had Prince Edward and Richarde his brother; but with what kinde of death these sely [innocent] chyldren wer executyd yt is not certanely known. But king Richard, delyveryd by this fact from his care and feare, kept the slaughter not long secret, who, within a few days after, permyttyd the rumor of ther death to go abrode, to thintent (as we may well beleve) that after the people understoode no yssue male of king Edward to be now left alyve, they might with better mynde and good will beare and sustayne his government. But whan the fame of this notable fowle act was dispersyd throwgh the realme, so great griefe stroke generally to the hartes of all men, that the same, subdewing all feare, they wept every wher...

There is obviously a problem with the reliability of the descriptions of the disappearance of the princes, a problem that becomes even more acute when other accounts are considered. If there was such great general horror at the death of the princes why at Richard's reception at York, which followed immediately after, (according to Vergil) did the people extol him above the skies? Furthermore, it would make no sense for Richard to kill the princes so soon after his coronation, putting at stake his popularity with the nobles and people. It is also highly unlikely that Richard himself would allow the rumour of their deaths to go abroad, for it would not take much political intelligence to realise that being associated in any way with the murder would cause significant damage to his reputation and support.

And even if there was a confession, confessions in Henry's reign were hardly reliable. Even the famous confession by Perkin Warbeck has been shown by Ann Wroe to be of very questionable veracity.[8]

Some writers confess ignorance of the murderer's identity, some blame Richard, some Buckingham. The accounts, which conflict in almost every detail, when taken together give an impression of being based on no reliable evidence.

Mancini carefully avoids implicating Richard, admitting that he lacks the evidence even to confirm Edward's death. [9]

> *[The princes] were withdrawn into the inner apartments of the Tower proper, and day by day began to be seen more rarely behind the bars and windows, till at length they ceased to appear altogether. The physician Argentine [later appointed as physician to Henry's heir, Prince Arthur], the last of his attendants whose services the king enjoyed, reported that the young king, like a victim prepared for sacrifice, sought remission of his sins by daily confession and penance, because he believed that death was facing him...I have seen many men burst into tears and lamentations when mention was made of him after his removal from men's sight; and already there was a suspicion that he had been done away with. Whether, however, he has been done away with, and by what matter of death, so far I have not discovered.*

The Croyland chronicler only repeats a rumour that they had met some sort of violent fate. Rous gives a very brief account, but blames Richard.[10]

> *[Richard imprisoned his lord King Edward V...together with his brother Richard...[It] was afterwards known to very few by what manner of death they had suffered. The usurper King Richard III then ascended the throne of the slaughtered children...He received his lord*

> *King Edward V blandly, with embraces and kisses, and within about three months or a little more he killed him together with his brother.*

The chronicler known as Vitellius does likewise.[11]

> *[Richard] also put to deth the ij children of kyng Edward, for whiche cavse he lost the hertes of the people. And therevpon many Gentlemen entendid his destruccion.*

However, it is clear that some writers in their determination to discredit Richard cannot agree whether it was the taking the throne or the murder of his nephews that was the principal reason for his loss of support.

The *Historical Notes of a London Citizen* adds to the confusion, by naming Buckingham as the instigator of the plan to murder the boys.[12]

> *...this year [1483] King Edward V, late called Prince of Wales and Richard Duke of York his brother, King Edward IV's sons were put to death in the Tower be vise [on the advice or by the plan] of the Duke of Buckingham.*

Unintentionally, Commines neatly presents the difficulty in determining what actually happened, for he first blames Richard. [13]

> *...this bloody King Richard who had so barbarously murdered his nephews.*

> *...the barbarous designs of the duke who murdered his nephews.*

But unable, it seems to remember what he had written elsewhere, he then blames Buckingham.[14]

> King Richard did not last long; nor did the Duke of Buckingham, who had put the two children to death, for a few days later King Richard had Buckingham put to death.

Diego de Valera wrote to Ferdinand and Isabella.[15]

> ...it is sufficiently well known to your royal majesty that this Richard killed two innocent nephews of his to whom the realm belonged after his brother's life; but for all that King Edward was waging war in Scotland, while Richard stayed in England, it is alleged that there he had them murdered with poison.

Obviously the difficulty of placing any credence in this is that it completely contradicts accepted facts, for he has Edward waging war in Scotland while Richard remained in England, changing the roles of the two brothers. Moreover, he states clearly that the princes were killed by poison, a method not generally considered by other writers, and he stretches the reader's credulity in having the boys killed while Edward was still alive. Of course, this was written after Henry's accession and so he probably accepted some of the many and contradictory rumours circulating at the time, being generally unconcerned about their strict accuracy, provided they were sufficient damning of Richard's reputation.

There is also Guillame de Rocheforts' speech to the Estates General, in 1484 when he was chancellor in which he claimed that the throne of England had been given to the murderer of Edward IV's sons.

A further account appears in *The Great Chronicle of London*. However, if this account is to be credited, the princes could not have been killed before or even shortly after Richard's accession, for they were seen playing in the grounds of the Tower during 1483 and rumours of their deaths did not surface until after Easter of the following year.[16]

> *[During 1483] the children of King Edward were seen shooting and playing in the garden of the Tower at sundry times. All the winter season [1483-4] the land was in good quiet, but after Easter there was much whispering among the people that the king had put the children of King Edward to death.*
>
> *Word sprang quickly of [Henry Tudor who] made speedy provision to come to England to claim the crown as his right, considering the death of King Edward's children, of whom as then men feared not only to say that they were rid out of this world. But of the manner of their deaths were many opinions, for some said they were murdered between two feather beds, some said they were drowned in malmsey [wine], and some said they were pierced with a venomous poison. But howsoever they were put to death, certain it was that before that day they were departed from this world, of which cruel deed Sir James Tyrell was reported to be the doer, but others put weight upon an old servant of King Richard's...*

This account, manifestly biased towards Henry, will hardly do for a number of reasons. The deaths of the children again are being used to provide a spurious justification for the invasion of Henry VII, who, far from being able to claim *"the crown as his right"*, had at best an extremely weak claim. However, it gave the appearance of justification for those who rose up in rebellion against the anointed king, Richard. The account clearly contradicts that of Mancini who had the children behind bars after the death of Hastings, not playing in the garden.

Fabian here seeks to confirm Richard's guilt by finding a connection with Buckingham's treason, but again there is no evidence of this.[17]

> *In this yere [1483-4] the foresayd grudge encreasinge, and the more for asmoche as the common fame went that kynge Richarde hadde within the Tower put vnto scerte deth the ii. sonnes of his boder Edwarde the iiii. For the wiche, and other causes hadde within the brest of thye duke of Bukkyngham, the sayd duke, in secrete maner,*

conspyred agayne hym, and allyed hym with dyuerse gentylmen, to the ende to bryng his purpose aboute.

Bacon heard rumours during the reign of Henry VII that one or both survived. In fact the claim of that famous pretender to the throne, Perkin Warbeck, could hardly have been given any credence at all unless people believed that it was least possible that he could be the rightful heir.

Those spreading the rumours about the princes' murder seem to have had no evidence whatsoever, since there are conflicting accounts of the deaths and of who the murderer was. If it were certain that Richard had been involved, one would expect that there would be definite evidence at least as to the manner of their deaths, but the boys are variously said to have been drowned in malmsey wine, starved, poisoned, stabbed, suffocated in a chest or smothered with their own bedclothes. William Rastell who was responsible for publishing More's account provided two differing versions of their deaths. In the first he states that one had his throat cut while the other was smothered, their bodies being disposed of at sea in a chest; in the other both boys were tricked into clambering into a chest which was then locked and buried under some stairs before being thrown into *"black depes"*.

Much has been made of the discovery of the skeletons of two children discovered in a wooden chest about ten feet underground while a staircase leading to a chapel in the White Tower was being demolished in the Tower in 1674. In 1678 these were placed in an urn in Henry VII's chapel in Westminster Abbey, and then in 1933 were submitted for a forensic examination, but the report failed to confirm whether the skeletons were male or female, although their age would be consistent with that of the princes. At some future date a DNA test will probably settle the matter. It has been regarded as significant the skeletons were discovered under a staircase, since this is where More indicated they were initially buried. However, not only is More alone in asserting this, but if his account is to be believed these skeletons cannot be the princes, as he goes on to say that they were moved from this place to a place unknown. Even were the skeletons to be proved to be those of the princes, we should be no closer to identifying their murderer. It is unlikely that forensic science will, at least in the foreseeable future, be able to determine the exact year in which they died and should this ever be possible it will still give no clue as to the hand by which they met their deaths. It must, therefore, be concluded that the skeletons neither prove nor disprove Richard's guilt.

There is some evidence which might point to Richard's innocence, though it is hardly conclusive. In Richard's wardrobe accounts under the heading concerning the materials delivered for the coronation there is an entry which runs: *"To Lorde Edward, son of the late Kyng Edward the Fourthe, for his apparaill and array..."*. It seems that this must refer to Richard's coronation and not the one planned for Edward, as he is designated *"Lord"* and the entry is sandwiched between entries for the *"King"* and *"Queen"* which can only refer to Richard and Anne. This being the case, plans must have been made for Edward to attend the coronation, with a number of expensively dressed supporters, and there to be given a place of honour.

The Harleian manuscript has two relevant entries.[18]

a) 18 July 1483: wages authorised to be paid to fourteen men for their services to Edward IV and to *"Edward the Bastard late called Edward V"*.

b) 9th March 1485: Henry Davy was given a *warrant "to deliver to John Goddeslande, footman unto the lord Bastard, two doublets of silk, one jacket of silk, one gown of cloth and two bonnets"*.

(a) seems to refer to Edward V, implying that he was still alive, but as the warrant was issued before the payment it does not preclude the possibility that by this date he was dead, and (b) could refer to Richard, Edward's younger brother, but this is not certain, as this Tower Wardrobe account might instead be referring to Richard's own illegitimate son.

There exists a letter from Richard to his chancellor, the Bishop of Lincoln dated 29 July 1483.

> ...*whereas we understand that certain persons of such as of late had taken upon them the fact of an enterprise, as we doubt not you have heard, be attached and in ward, we desire and will that you do make our letters of commission to such persons as by you and our council shall be advised for to sit upon them and to proceed to the due execution of our laws in that behalf.*

This tantalising letter unfortunately does not state what the *"enterprise"* was. If it refers to the murder of the princes, Richard is being especially circumspect, not wanting to reveal too much about such a delicate matter, but obviously he wants the Council to deal with it and punish the offenders.

Hard evidence being unavailable, there is only circumstantial evidence left upon which to begin to make a judgement. The obvious first question is whether or not Richard had anything to gain by the murders – to which the answer is probably "yes". If they were killed after Buckingham's rebellion it could have been in response to the fear that they would provide a focus for dissatisfied elements in the country. If somehow the Woodvilles were to have regained control of one or both boys Richard might have been in serious political danger, especially since a decision by one parliament declaring them illegitimate might easily be reversed by another when there was a change in the balance of power. However, it is also possible to argue that Richard had relatively little to gain and much to lose by the death of the princes, for the threat of powerful nobles rallying to a possible claimant to the throne would not be removed by their murder. Clarence's son had a claim and, although he had been disbarred by reason of his father's treason, the pragmatism of power-brokers, which was often a driving force in English politics, could have ensured a reversal of his attainder. It would seem at the least inconsistent on the part of Richard to have had one brother's sons murdered while letting this nephew live. If Richard felt his position threatened by the princes, despite their declared illegitimacy, he must surely have felt almost equally threatened by Edward.

The son of Richard's sister could also maintain a claim, while if Edward's daughters could be married to foreign princes, support might rally to them. The problem of supposing that Richard had the princes killed is that we must then assume that he was willing to replace a problem that he had within his control with problems that could be less easily countered. Richard, although not a subtle politician, certainly possessed political understanding, and he must have been aware that by murdering the boys he might further alienate the Woodville faction, placing more obstacles in the way of reconciliation and of his security.

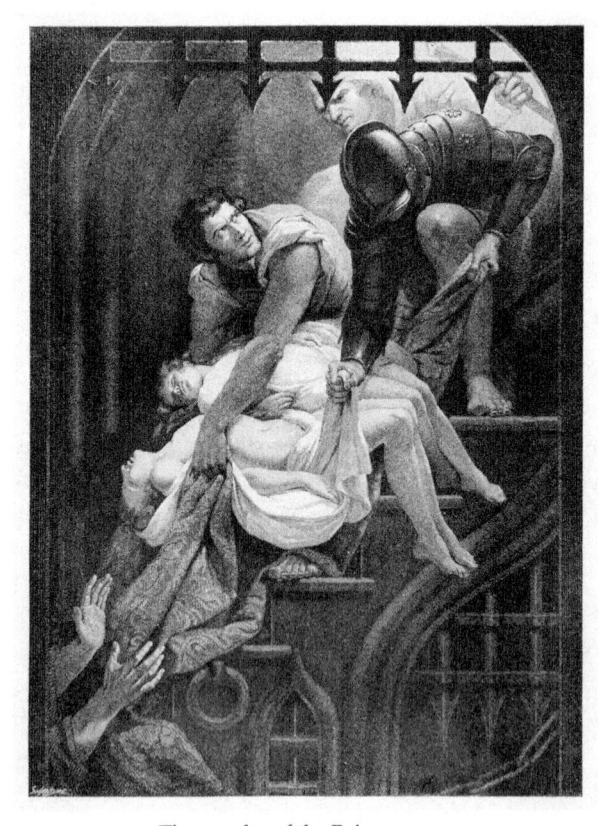

The murder of the Princes

From all of the accounts, one thing is obvious: there is no direct evidence linking Richard to the disappearance of the princes. The conflicting, contradictory and unreliable evidence, even concerning the most obvious details, does not allow the reader to assume Richard's guilt, though neither does it prove his innocence. Certainly the test of *beyond reasonable doubt* for English criminal law is by no means satisfied. From these fundamental uncertainties, it seems that those who accuse Richard of murder do so lacking any evidence, especially since some of the contemporary chroniclers, even including those generally hostile to Richard, believed that the murderer remained unknown. The fact that rumours about Richard's involvement were circulating widely at the time does not allow us to assume Richard's guilt; people in every age know only too well how false and malicious rumours can develop, gaining the currency of credibility by reason of their repetition. But relying on rumours as historical evidence is fraught with difficulties, not least of which is that, in this case, the accounts vary and are contradictory. More's warning that regarding the truth of their death *"some remain yet in doubt, whither they wer in his dayes destroyed or no"* is still pertinent today. If rumours be allowed to stand for evidence, who shall escape conviction?

Richard was not the only person with a motive for killing the princes. If, as is not unreasonable to suppose, the princes had survived Richard's reign, Henry VII had at least as much as Richard to gain by their deaths. His claim to the throne was by right of conquest, there being but the most tenuous of claims through the bloodlines; and so Henry, despite his marriage into the House of York would have felt as vulnerable, if support had gathered in support of Edward, as he would feel later facing the challenge of Warbeck. It is also intriguing that, if in 1486 Henry did give two royal pardons to James Tyrell, there is the possibility that Tyrell murdered the boys in his reign rather than Richard's. Moreover, there is a difficulty in supposing that Tyrell carried out the murder on Richard's instruction. Tyrell seems to have been implicated initially because he made the journey from York to London to collect materials for the presentation of the Prince of Wales in York which was to take place on 8 September. In order to return in time for this he would have had to leave London several days earlier than he did. However, the Croyland chronicler assumes that they were still alive at the time of the presentation, and that the rebellion was being fomented in the south and west had as one of its principal aims their release.

If an indication of Richard's guilt is his failure to quash the rumours of their deaths by presenting them in public, it is an indication of Henry's guilt that at no point - except for an oblique reference in the Act of Attainder to the shedding of infants' blood - did he claim that Richard had murdered them, which is odd, since if he could substantiate the claim it would have strengthened his position in two ways: he could be seen as the man who had saved the country from the sort of tyranny that preyed on the innocent; and their deaths would have bolstered his position since his wife, Elizabeth, sister of princes could claim to be the rightful heir of Edward IV. If the bodies found under the stairs could be proved to those of the princes (which we have already seen to be problematic), Henry would be exonerated, as the reported ages of the skeletons indicate children too young to be Henry's victims.

Another obvious suspect is Buckingham. The boys would have provided a threat to him if he had rebelled successfully against Richard and claimed the throne. However, if Henry never directly accused Richard, Richard never accused Buckingham, though exposure of Buckingham's guilt would have strengthened his position. There is also the problem of access. Buckingham would have had to find a way past those guarding the boys in order to have them murdered, and it seems improbable that he would have been able to do this, or having done it prevented it from coming to Richard's knowledge.

Philippa Gregory, who stresses the pivotal roles played by women during this turbulent period, believes Henry Tudor's mother is a principal suspect. Margaret Beaufort, ruthless and obsessively ambitious for her son, perceived the princes as an obstacle to Henry's eventual succession, and so, gaining access to the Tower either through her husband, Stanley, or her co-conspirator, Buckingham, may well have contrived their murder.

Whoever was responsible for their deaths an appeal to political exigency or to the differing attitudes of the time would provide insufficient excuse for such a crime. It was powerfully argued by

Philippe Ariès that children were largely disregarded in the Middle Ages since the high infant mortality rate, among other things, prevented parents from investing too much emotional capital in children, who might well not survive to adulthood.[19] However, it seems clear that this thesis is mistaken. The medieval period had a somewhat ambiguous view of children, an attitude that should not surprise us, since our society too presents conflicting images of children ranging from the sweet and innocent to the violent, rude and unruly. If the Middle Ages condemned childish misbehaviour it also elevated childlike innocence to the status of necessary virtue. In his Boy Bishop sermon of 1558, preached at Gloucester, John Stubbs condemns the behaviour of the children he sees around him. He says that it was a wonder to him to see *"so many childer in years and so few innocents in maners"*. He warns that the children of the city can teach adults *"evill properties"*; the boys of the grammar schools are *"as evill or rather worse than the other…ripe and redy in all lewd libertie*; and the boys of the song school are so badly behaved that they *"never serve God nor our Lady with mattyns or with evynsong"*. Even a boy whom he picks out in the congregation who looks as though *"butter wolde not melt in his mouth"* would prove to be far from innocent if people knew what John Subbs knew about him. Rather than disregarding their children, Stubbs argues that parents presented the opposite vice: *"a folysh affection and a fond [doting/foolish] opinion in the parentes which very fondly seek the love of the child that knoweth not what love or dutye meaneth, that he might say 'I am father's boy' and 'I love father (mother) best'; to wyn this word, and the love of the child, the parents contend who shall make the most of the child and by these means no partye dare displease hym, say he or do he never so ongraciously, but both parties dandill hym and didill hym and pamper him and stroke his hedd and sett hym a hye bence and gyve him the swetyst soppe in the dish evyn when he lest desrve it"*. However, the churchmen used the slaughter of the children by Herod to reinforce the virtues of the innocence of children, an innocence that each person would require if they were desirous of entering the kingdom of heaven.

It is not too much to suppose that the rumours of the princes' deaths were fuelled by a love of sensation and sentiment, at least as far as young royals were concerned. In the previous century, underlying some of the resentments of the Peasants' Revolt in 1381 was the idea that the boy-king Richard II had been wickedly misled by his advisors. An age generally thought cruel by modern standards had a particularly soft spot for the idealised children of the royal household, even if everyone was all too aware of the failings of the real children they met in their everyday dealings. With that sort of sentiment, it is not difficult to understand how, when a rumour could be whipped up into a hysteria of moral outrage, a perpetrator would be sought, whether innocent or not: a reaction all too common in every age. Yet, if the princes were murdered, it is not sufficient to pass it off as a product of the cruelty of the age; it was clearly a heinous crime, regarded, then as now, as going beyond the boundaries of civilised behaviour.

Another theory is that at least one of the princes escaped from the Tower. Clearly the complete lack of any reliable evidence regarding the fate of the princes at the time lent credence to the claims of Lambert Simnel and Perkin Warbeck in the reign of Henry VII. Although the priest Richard Simon falsely claimed Simnel to be the son of Clarence, he had originally thought to present him as Edward IV's younger son, Richard.

Perkin Warbeck did claim that he was Richard, son of Edward IV, who, having been smuggled out of the Tower by one of his brother's murderers overcome with pity for the young boy, had promised this rescuer secrecy for a number of years. It is generally considered that Warbeck was an impostor who eventually gave Henry VII little option but to execute him. Though undoubtedly the political convenience of the claims allowed some supporters to overcome their doubts, the ability of Warbeck to gather wide, influential and highly placed support, would suggest a widespread uncertainty over the fate of the boys.

Jack Leslau has proposed an ingenious theory to explain the disappearance of the princes, after considering one of pictures of Thomas More's family, based on a sketch by Holbein. He believes that both princes survived Richard's reign, were smuggled out of the Tower and were given new identities on the understanding with Henry VII that they would abandon any claim to the throne and that Henry would marry their sister Elizabeth of York. Edward was given the identity of Sir Edward Guildford, son of the comptroller to the royal household, and Richard became Dr John Clement, later the president of the Royal College of Physicians. Dr Clement, who appears in the portrait of the More family, since he was a member of his household, is a man whose rise to importance is somewhat mysterious. The position of president of the Royal College of Physicians was in the gift of the monarch, but in the entire history of the Royal Society this is the only president for whom there is no signature, portrait, or records, and about whose family nothing is known. Leslau believes that the tomb of Sir Edward Guildford's daughter in Chelsea Old Church, London supports his claim since it names her as a princess. Leslau contends that the More portrait holds further clues, but his interpretation is very controversial and does no more than provide disputed circumstantial evidence. It would also be somewhat strange for More, or a member of his household, to reveal such a potentially damaging secret to be encoded in a painting, bearing in mind that the code, if it is capable of being understood now, would have been far more easily read at the time of the painting. Furthermore, it would have been a desperately dangerous move to keep the princes physically so close to the centre of power where there was every chance that they might be recognised. Professor Pollard seems in the right of it when he describes this theory as *"a brilliant flight of fancy"*.

Leslau's theory highlights the real problem with deciding the fate of the Princes in the Tower: lack of evidence, not only lack of evidence pointing to a murderer, but lack of evidence that they were murdered at all. All that is left is circumstantial evidence, evidence that is both contradictory and inconclusive. Thus the way is open to a wide range of plausible - and implausible - theories.

Shortly after his description of the death of the princes, Vergil indulges in a typical piece of criticism.[20]

> *[He began] to take on hand a certain new form of life, and to give the show and countenance of a good man, whereby he might be accounted*

> *more righteous, more mild, better affected to the commonalty, and more liberal, especially towards the poor. [So that he] first might merit pardon for his offences at God's hand, than after appease partly the envy of man and procure himself goodwill, he began many works public and private...But anon after it appeared evident that fear, which seldom causes continuance of dutiful dealing, made Richard so suddenly good, forasmuch as the bountifulness of the man, being but counterfeit, waxed coldly again.*

Both Vergil and the Croyland chronicler do not hesitate to make definite statements about Richard's thoughts and motivation, things that can be but mere guesses, but imputing unworthy motives to him.

While Richard was staying in Lincoln on his return journey from York, though probably already aware of the conspiracy, he gained confirmed intelligence that the south and west were rebelling, led by Buckingham in alliance with the Lancastrians and Elizabeth Woodville with her faction. The *Croyland Chronicle* states that foremost in the minds of the rebels was the imprisonment of the princes in the Tower, and their aim was *"to deliver them from this captivity"*.[21] However, when the rumour of the princes' deaths was spread abroad, the aim became to support Henry Tudor's bid for the throne. It is obvious why the Lancastrians would support Henry, but Elizabeth's support could surely only have been gained if she no longer entertained any hopes of one of her sons being crowned; so presumably she believed them both to be dead; not that her belief is proof in itself. However, a marriage of her daughter Elizabeth to Henry would potentially re-establish the Woodvilles at the heart of power.

The motivation behind Buckingham's rebellion is another mystery to add to the rest of those surrounding Richard's life and reign. Although there have been several attempts to unravel this unstable, proud lord's reasons for turning on Richard, none is properly supported by evidence and all remain unconvincing. It has been suggested that the persuasive and crafty Bishop Morton, who was Buckingham's prisoner and who harboured Lancastrian sympathies, somehow managed to persuade

Buckingham that it lay to his advantage to change his allegiance to Henry. There is some evidence for this in the *Croyland Chronicle*, which tries to justify Buckingham's role by suggesting that he joined the rebellion only after the princes were presumed dead. It goes on to state that *"a message was sent to him [Henry] by the Duke of Buckingham on the advice of the lord bishop of Ely, his prisoner at Brecknock, inviting him to hasten into the kingdom of England as fast as he could reach the shore to marry Elizabeth, the dead king's daughter, and with her, at the same time, take possession of the whole kingdom"*. Polydore Vergil gives an alternative motivation, supposing that Buckingham believed that he had been insufficiently rewarded for his support.[22]

> [Buckingham] demandyd of king Richerd that part of therle of Herefoordes patrimony that to him by right of inheritance was dew. To this king Richerd, who supposyd the matter to have bene now forgotten, ys reported to have awnswered forthwith in great rage: 'What now, duke Henry, will yow chalenge unto you that right of Henry the Fourth wherby he wickedly usurped the crowne, and so make open for yourself the way thereunto?' Which king Richerd's awnswer settlyd depe into the dukes breste, who from that time furth, movyd muche with ire and indignation, began to devyse by what meane he might thrust owt that ungratefull man from the royall seat for whose cause he had right often done many thinges agaynste his owne conscyence otherwise than before God he lawfully might.

Yet Richard had made generous gifts of land and titles to him. He even supported him in his claim for the remaining half of the Hereford inheritance, which was awaiting parliament's approval. Even if Buckingham believed that this would not be forthcoming it hardly provided him with a grievance against Richard. Vergil makes Buckingham, not Morton, the instigator of the plot to support Henry in his claim to the throne and conveniently for Morton, who was favoured by Henry VII, paints him as an honourable man, fearful of being a party to treason.

> *Heare the while of his tary, provokyd partly by freshe memory of the late receavyd injury, partly repenting that hitherto of himself hee had not resystyd king Richerdes evell enterprise, but had much furtheryd the same, he resolvyd to seperate himself from him (though in dede he showld so have doon in the begynyng), and to bring to passe the thing which he long revolvyd in mynde: and so he began to discover his intent to John bishop of Ely, whom (as we before remembryd) he had in Brechnoch castle. The bisshop syuspecting treason, demandeth why he goeth abowt that matter, and prayeth to do him no harm; afterward whan he understood his just cause of hatred, which king Richerd had well deservyd long ago, he refusyd not to conferre of the conspiracy. Than the duke unfoldyd all thynges to the bisshop of Ely, and dyscoveryd himself wholly, shewing how he had devised the meane wherby both the bloode of king Edward and of Henry the Sixth that year was remaining, being conjoignyd by affinytie, might be restoryd to the dominion dew unto both ther progenynes. The meane was this, that Henry erle of Richemond, who (as the report went) was, after knowledge of king Edwardes death, delyverd by Francys duke of Brytayne owt of prison, might be sent for in hast possible...*

There is much that is obviously questionable in this account. It paints an almost saintly picture of Bishop Morton, who was no saint, but who was important to Henry VII. It is inconsistent in ascribing thoughts to Buckingham, for on the one hand Buckingham is said to have conceived the plot as result of his snub and his newly awakened conscience, while on the other the plot is said to have been something he had considered for a long time. The justification of seeing two royal lines combined in Henry is an obvious attempt to ascribe a moral purpose to Morton, who must have realised that Henry had no legitimate claim to the throne through his family. Similarly, Vergil tries to throw a halo over Morton's head by claiming that he, being worried by treason, hopes Buckingham will do no harm, but then changes his mind when Buckingham reveals Richard's wickedness. This has the odour of fake eulogy. Morton would have been well aware of most, if not all, of

Richard's supposed evil deeds, not least because he was imprisoned for his own part in a plot against Richard. He hardly needed a moral justification from Buckingham to fuel his hatred of Richard. Those who see a more honourable side to him have suggested that Buckingham rebelled because of his disquiet or disgust at the murder of the princes; yet, it is more likely that Buckingham conceived his plot before the rebellion, while the princes were still living. Audrey Williamson believes that Buckingham wrote to Henry Tudor on 24 September 1483 to encourage him to invade, giving as one of the aims of the invasion the freeing of the princes.[23] It is not impossible that Buckingham rebelled because he aimed at the throne himself; after all, his claim through a son of Edward III was better than Henry Tudor's and in fact better than all but Richard's own and that of his son. Perhaps he considered that pretending support for Henry would give him thebacking he needed from the Woodvilles and the Lancastrians. Perhaps he believed that Henry could always be disposed of later, assuming that his own, better claim would not allow him to ascend the throne by more legitimate means.

More believed that it was ambition driving Buckingham.[24]

> *Very trouth it is, the duke was an high minded man, and euyll could beare the glory of an other, so that I haue heard of som that said thei saw it, that the duke at such time as the crown was first set upon the protectors hed, his eye could not abide the sight thereof, but wried his hed an other way.*

But, as we have already noted, More is hardly a reliable source.

The strength of Henry's claim to the throne does not bear scrutiny. There were two possible lines for such a claim. Henry V had married Katherine de Valois, daughter of the French King Charles VI. The son of this union was Henry VI. When Henry V died early, Katherine, having conducted an affair with Owen Tudor gave birth to the illegitimate Edmund, the father of Henry Tudor. Even if, as Owen claimed, he and Katherine had secretly married before the birth it would give Henry no claim since his father was merely half-brother to Henry VI by a common mother. He had no affinity in blood to Henry V.

The other line is somewhat more complicated. Since his mother was Margaret Beaufort, Henry could trace his line through the Beauforts to John of Gaunt, who was the second surviving son of Edward III. However, all four Beaufort children were the result of an affair between John of Gaunt and Katherine Swinford, although John and Katherine did later marry. Thus, all the Beaufort children were illegitimate. However, their status was complicated first by a decree approved by King Richard and the Pope making them legitimate, and then by Henry IV once more declaring them illegitimate. It followed that the Beaufort line could not provide a claim to the throne.

Margaret Beaufort

Following the shipwreck after his flight in 1471, Henry had been effectively the prisoner of the Duke Francis of Brittany and he became, unsurprisingly, the focus of political manoeuvrings. Henry wished the

Duke to grant permission for an invasion of England to restore the House of Lancaster; his mother had tried negotiating for his return to court and for a reconciliation with the House of York. Francis had his own agenda and saw in Henry a means of playing France and England against each other. Part of this plan was to try to persuade Richard to send him troops to counter the French threat, on the grounds that, if Brittany were defeated by France, Richard would be placed in a worse position, as it would encourage the French to sponsor an invasion led by Henry. With Richard refusing to engage in this plan, Francis himself began to support Henry's invasion, aided by money from Henry's supporters in England. Any notion that Henry invaded as a result of the supposed murder of the princes is mere fantasy and an attempt to credit Henry with more noble motives than his real desire, which was to usurp a throne. That this was his true motivation is obvious not only because he had long since planned the campaign, but also because no one dealing with the political realities of the situation was going to mount an invasion simply because he felt revulsion at the death of two young boys. Henry's invasion, the culmination of years of plotting, was not the fruit of moral outrage.

If Simon Stallworth, writing shortly after Hasting's execution, is to be believed Hasting's men had been transferring their allegiance to Buckingham, and money had been sent to Henry for some time by members of the Woodville faction as well as by some Lancastrians. It was planned that the South would rise at the same time as Buckingham was to lead forces from Wales, while Henry was to invade from Brittany.

Typically, Richard wasted no time responding to Buckingham's rebellion. From Grantham he sent a letter requesting the Great Seal so that he might counter the *"rebelled and traytoure the Duc of Bukingham"* and *"resiste and withstonde his malicious purpose"*.[25] Richard's dismay and anger at such treachery is clear from the postscript penned in his own hand. *"Here loved be God ys all well & trewly determynd & for to resyste the malysse of Hym that hadde best cause to be trewe the duc of Bokyngham the most untrewe creature lyvyng whom with Godes grace we shall not be long tyll we wyll be in that parties & subdewe hys malys. We you assure was never fals traytor better purvayde [provided] for, as berrerr [bearer], Gloucestre, shall shewe you.* As far as it is possible to discern such things, Richard seems to have been quite genuinely surprised and angered by Buckingham's treachery, seeing no reason why he should behave in such a fashion. It is the outburst of, if not an innocent man, or at least a man who believes himself without fault in the matter.

Within two weeks Richard had stationed himself at Leicester and, continuing to act quickly, collected his forces and moved against the rebels. Although there was support for the rebels in the southern and western counties, importantly, the midlands and north stood with him.

Since London was safe, Richard moved against Buckingham's army, while others disrupted his supply lines and destroyed the bridges across the Severn. Although Richard had the military advantage, his success was secured by the weather. In the storm it rained so hard that, in the absence of bridges, the Severn was impassable, Buckingham's supplies were further disrupted, causing mass desertions, and Henry's fleet was scattered. Despite reaching Plymouth himself, Henry, on hearing the news of Buckingham's failure, returned to Brittany. Buckingham's capture reveals the treachery of the time. Although he had sought refuge in the cottage of a loyal supporter, this supporter's loyalty was insufficient to withstand either the temptations of a reward, or fear of the danger in which he had been placed, and the duke was surrendered to the sheriff of Shropshire. Bishop Morton fled to Flanders and Buckingham, tried by the Vice-Constable, was executed in Salisbury on 2 November. The Croyland chronicler writes of what followed.[26]

> *...the king proceeded with all his army towards the western parts of the kingdom, where all his enemies had made a stand, with the exception of those who had come from Kent, and were at Guildford, awaiting the issue of events. Proceeding onwards, he arrived at the city of Exeter; upon which, being struck with extreme terror at his approach, Peter Courteney, bishop of Exeter, as well as Thomas, marquis of Dorset, and various other nobles of the adjacent county, who had taken part in the rebellion, repaired to the sea-side; and those*

> among them who could find ships in readiness, embarked, and at length arrived at the wished-for shores of Brittany. Others, for a time trusting to the fidelity of friends, and concealing themselves in secret spots, afterwards betook themselves to the protection of holy places.

On Richard's return to London several of the leading conspirators and some others, perhaps members of his own household, having been executed, parliament denounced all the exiles as traitors and their goods confiscate.

Richard had put down the rebellion, yet it was obvious that all was not well. The north remained loyal enough, but the south had yet either to be won over or subdued. Furthermore, Henry Tudor, now safely back in Brittany, had emerged as a clear claimant for the throne, with continued support from the Woodville and Lancastrian factions.

Buckingham was the only great noble to have been involved in the rebellion; the others either supported Richard or bided their time. Richard's generosity and fair-mindedness are revealed in the way he dealt with Buckingham's widow, another Woodville. He discharged Buckingham's debts and, after granting her a pension, permitted her to seek sanctuary with Elizabeth, her sister, at Westminster. Even Lady Stanley, a principal conspirator, was treated more than mercifully: her lands being granted to her husband and not forfeited, she was then placed in his care. Later her attainder was removed. Stanley, far from being punished for his wife's part in the rebellion, was rewarded with Buckingham's previous title of constable of England for life, together with a number of important lands.

It is unsurprising that Richard, having faced rebellion in the south, and fearing for the security of his reign, turned in large part to the more loyal northern lords, whom he rewarded with land and titles. It was not that the southern lords were completely ignored, but the balance was now clearly northwards. Those who had risen against Richard, in spite of being restored to some of their lands and pardoned for supporting the rebellion, must have been aware that they could hardly be considered trustworthy any longer; and, given the relatively unstable state of the realm, could not expect to be promoted to positions of trust and power. Those in the south naturally resented the intrusion of the northern lords, but Richard decided that this resentment was the price worth paying for a greater control of the more disloyal part of the country.

The Croyland chronicler was dismayed at the turn of events, but then he was writing from a southerner's point of view.[27]

> *After these events [Buckingham's rebellion], the king gradually lessened his army, and dismissing those who had been summoned from the northern borders to take part in the expedition, came to London, having triumphed over his enemies without fighting a battle, but at an expense not less than if two armies had fought hand to hand. Thus was commenced the waste in a short time, of those most ample treasures which king Edward supposed he should leave behind him for quite a different purpose...What immense estates and patrimonies were collected into this king's treasury in consequence of this measure! [the attainders of lords spiritual and temporal and commoners] all of which he distributed among his northern adherents, whom he planted in every spot throughout his dominions, to the disgrace and lasting and loudly expressed sorrow of all the people in the south, who daily longed more and more for the hoped-for return of their ancient rulers, rather than the present tyranny of these people.*

Leaving aside the, perhaps, deliberate error that Richard squandered the wealth accumulated by Edward, when in fact Edward left the Crown with little wealth and much of what remained was stolen by Elizabeth and Edward Woodville, it seems that the Croyland Chronicler is somewhat unguarded in revealing his southern bias. There does not seem to be any evidence that the new northern lords were any harsher than their predecessors, only that the southern lords, unsurprisingly, disliked the promotion of northerners.

It is not fair to say that Richard promoted only northerners; southerners were promoted too. Neither did Richard seek to "pack" his government with those newly appointed loyalists, for the established lords still held sway. The protests of the southerners can be seen as the sort of cries and outrage that are only to be expected when privileges long taken for granted are removed or placed under threat. However, Richard did rely mainly on northerners for his household, men such as Sir Robert Brackenby, although William Catesby and Sir James Tyrell were both southerners.

In order to stabilise the south Richard also decided to appoint a number of military officers who had proved their loyalty in the uprising to positions of authority as sheriffs and constables. All this was in order to pave the way for a dutiful, just and fair administration of the realm.

It has been claimed that the introduction of Richard's northern supporters was but a temporary expedient, designed solely to deal with the unrest in the south, but his rule would not endure long enough to show the truth of the matter.

-7-

Governing the Kingdom

Richard desired to be known as a dutiful and just king. If it were not for the successful invasion of Henry Tudor, which curtailed his brief reign, rather than being labelled as "Dick the Bad", he might have been judged by history as the reforming king, benevolent and able, who having united the country riven by powerful factions, and resolving the troubles bequeathed by Edward IV, invited England into the early modern age. However, because he was toppled by a usurping regime keen to discredit his reign, before he could establish his rule, little that Richard achieved could satisfy some of his critics and every action, no matter how beneficial, might be interpreted to his detriment. A typical example of this can be found in Vergil.[1]

> *Thus when king Richard was spoken of at all hands, and though hee [was] not ignorant from whom these speeches dyd procede, yeat for all that durst not by violence revenge the same, supposing yt an unwise part not to beare soom time with suche as towld him of his fault, he fell agane from so great felycytie into a feare and heavynes of hart, and, because he could not reform the thing that was past, he determynyd to abholishe by all dewtyfulnes the note of infamy wherewith his honor was staynyd, and to geave suche hope of his good government that from thenceforth no man showld be hable to lay any calamytie that might happen to the commonwealth unto his charge.*

So neatly does Vergil condemn. Richard shows *"dutifulness"* and gives of *"good government"* merely to extirpate his former sins, and just to bide his time. But Vergil has more. If Richard's actions themselves could not be criticised, then Vergil simply proclaims them to be the works of a hypocrite and opportunist, ignoring the fact that Richard had exhibited precisely the same concern for good government and justice while in the north:

> *But hard yt ys to alter the naturall disposition of ones minde, and suddaynly to exterp the thing therin settlyd by dayly conversation. And so, whether yt were for that cause, or (as the brute commonly goeth) because he now repented of his evell dedes, he began afterward to take on hand a certane new forme of lyfe, and to geave the shew and cowtenance of a good man, wherby he might be accowntyd more righteous, more mylde, better affectyd to commonalitie, and more lyberall especially toward the powr; and so first might meryte pardon for his offences at Gods hand; than after appease partly thenvy of man, and procure himself good will, he began many woorkes as well publick and private, which (being prevented by death before his time) he perfyted not.*

Then Vergil neatly develops his theme about the underlying wickedness of Richard by describing it re-emerging:

> *But anon after yt appearyd evident that feare, which seldom causeth continewance of dewtifull dealing, made king Richard so suddainly good, for as much as the boutyfulness of the man beinge but counterfayt waxed cold agane quickly; by reason wherof all his proposyd practises began straightway to coom to naught.*

Nevertheless, we should look at Richard's reign in a more dispassionate light and consider his achievements. At the beginning of the year he again refused a gift, this time from the grateful people of Canterbury. In Council he made Southwark a part of the liberty of the

City and gave £10,000 for strengthening its defences. In the parliament, opened on 23 January 1484, which enacted the *Titulus Regius*, Richard promoted a series of progressive and improving measures, and had an act of attainder passed condemning the rebels who had taken part in the recent uprising.

He abolished benevolences a most unpopular form of taxation which had brought men to *"their almost utter destruction"* and had compelled others to *"break up their households, and to live in great penury and wretchedness"*. Thus, in effect, he abandoned the raising of taxes without the consent of parliament. It had been the custom to imprison suspects before trial, but a new measure, reflecting his interest in the law, allowed justices of the peace to release such people, at their discretion, on bail. The same measure forbade officers from confiscating the goods *"of any person arrested and imprisoned for suspicion of felony before that the same person, so arrested or imprisoned, be convicted or attainted of such felony according to law"*. He also tried to protect juries from intimidation and corruption, and amended land law so that buyers would be protected from the hidden defects in their titles. There is a hint that Richard, who owned a vernacular copy of the New Testament, was concerned to promote the spread of learning; resident foreigners, who were subject to import restrictions for other goods, were exempted from such restrictions for books and were allowed to trade freely.

He had already eased the problem of the less wealthy being denied justice by appointing John Haryngton to deal with *"the custody, registration and expedition of bills, requests and supplications of poor persons"*, and so established what was almost certainly the beginning of the court that was to become the Court of Requests, a court for poor people that processed cases relatively quickly and challenged the common law courts.

These measures are forward-looking, indicating not only Richard's interest in justice, but also a desire to improve and modernise. It is not possible to determine what other reforming legislation might have been enacted had Richard reigned for longer, but certainly this parliament set a promising precedent, giving a clear indication of one reason why the north which he had ruled effectively for a number of years was so supportive. Of course, it might well be argued that credit for this legislation ought at least to be shared with parliament itself; indeed it is difficult to apportion this credit. It is possible, nevertheless, to claim with some confidence that Richard set the tone and was probably the instigator and driver. If not everyone was pleased with the result, that is the price any reformer has to pay.

Even if the content is ignored, there is a further ground for seeing Richard's legislation as looking towards the future: for the first time statutes were drafted in English.

Perhaps it seemed to Richard that his attempts to pacify and unite the nation were bearing fruit when he successfully persuaded Elizabeth Woodville to release her daughters from sanctuary, symbolising a reconciliation with the Woodvilles. Richard made a solemn undertaking.[2]

> *Elizabeth, Cecille, Anne, Kateryn and Briggitte wolle come unto me out of the Saintwarie of Westminstre and be guyded, Ruled & demeaned after me, than I shalle see that they shalbe in suertie of their lyffes and also not suffer any maner hurt by any maner persone or persones to theim or any of theim in their bodies and persones to be done by wey of Ravisshement or defouling contrarie their willes, nor theim or any of theim, emprisone within the Toure of London or other prisone, but that I shalle puttheim in honest places of good name & fame, and theim honestly & curtesly shalle see to be foundene & entreated and to have alle thinges requisite & necessary for their exibicione and findinges as my kynneswomen.*

He went further, promising to find suitable marriages and settlements, not to punish them on the report of others without giving them a fair hearing and making a pension provision for Elizabeth herself.

It was suggested earlier that Elizabeth would only have supported Henry VII if she were sure her sons were dead. Yet, if she believed that Richard had been responsible for their deaths it might be thought strange that she should entrust the welfare of her daughters to him. It is unlikely that the strong-minded Elizabeth could be cowed into this, but perhaps being a calculating political manoeuvrer she thought that it were better to rely on a public promise of safety from Richard than to rely on the security of a sanctuary that might come to be regarded as less than sacrosanct. For his part, Richard gained not only an apparent reconciliation with the Woodvilles, but sufficient control over the girls to prevent them from marrying Henry Tudor.

His generosity to the University of Cambridge was acknowledged by the University on 14 March 1484 which thanked him because he *"lately, liberally, and devoutly founded an exhibition for four priests in the Queens College...and with the greatest kindness, bestowed and expended not a little money for the strength and ornament of the university, both in most graciously ratifying the privileges of the university, as also with the most devout intention founding and erecting the buildings of Kings College, the unparalleled ornament of all England".*[3]

In addition Queen Anne endowed Queens' College with *"great rents"*.

While politically things might have seemed to be swinging in Richard's favour, tragedy was to strike. The King and Queen who were at Nottingham were informed in April that Edward, Richard's one legitimate son, had died aged at just eleven years of age. He was buried at Sheriff Hutton. The reaction of Richard and Anne accords with emotions expressed at the imagined death of the Princes in the Tower, revealing again the sympathy that is commonly felt towards children. The Croyland chronicler recorded the sad event.[4]

> *...in the following month of April, on a day not very far distant from the anniversary of king Edward, this only son of his, in whom all the hopes of the royal succession, fortified with so many oaths, were centred, was seized with an illness of but short duration, and died at Middleham Castle, in the year of our Lord, 1484, being the first of the reign of the said king Richard. On hearing the news of this, at Nottingham, where they were then residing, you might have seen his*

> *father and mother in a state almost bordering on madness, by reason of their sudden grief.*

Richard suffered a second tragedy six months later when his wife, Anne, who was suffering from ill-health – probably tuberculosis -, died, in all likelihood hastened to her grave by the loss of her child.

It was not only at his son's death that Richard showed himself to have been a loving and devoted father; the accounts for Middleham show that he had taken care to provide well for the boy, authorising expenditure for everything from a feather and clothing to a primer (prayer book), psalter, and household expenses.

Richard, although perhaps not so adept at political manoeuvring as his brother had been, nevertheless did not let important lessons go unheeded. Edward had used Richard to secure his authority in the north, being ever-wary of those powerful northern lords, whose allegiance might at any time be brought into question. Edward had recognised that he could ill-afford to allow these lords to promote divisions in the kingdom. Richard, whose loyalty had been thoroughly tested, had been the ideal candidate to keep the north quiet and in control of the crown, and he had gained widespread and enthusiastic support from the northerners during this time. Nonetheless, he was sensible to the risks that might emerge if the Percys or the Stanleys decided to test their strength. And the loyalty of both Percy and Stanley might be doubted, Percy because he longed to recover his lost authority in the north and Stanley through his marriage to Margaret Beaufort, Henry Tudor's mother. To keep the northern lords in check and to promote good and effective government Richard established the Council of the North and retained of the wardenship of the west marches in his own hands.

The Council of the North, established in July 1484, was placed under the presidency of the Earl of Lincoln, his loyal nephew. Richard used money from his estates in the north to support this council, which was mandated to keep the region quiet. It was ordered to *"examine & ordre alle billes of compleyntes & other there before theym to be shewed...ordre and direct alle riotes, forcible entres, distresse takings, variaunces, debates &*

othere mysbehavors ayenst" the laws and peace.

By this means the power of the crown, which previously had to rely largely upon the government of the northern magnates was effectively extended. The security of the northern border with Scotland, however, lay outside its jurisdiction. This can be seen as part of Richard's wider strategy for governing a pacified realm. The council was also empowered to resist, withstand and punish any assemblies made contrary to the peace.

The parliament had given Richard the opportunity to reform part of the administration of justice, something which genuinely seems to have interested him. He wished for an efficient system, but also one that was just and free from corruption. He famously called all the justices to a meeting in the Star Chamber in order to pose them three questions about the administration of justice. In theory, at least, the judges dispensed the king's justice and Richard seems determined to see that it was administered to a high standard. He quoted cases and asked them three difficult questions concerning legal malpractice, being especially worried about the injustice occasioned by one case in particular, and concluded by reiterating his personal interest in the law: *"per justicios suos et legem suam unum est dicere"* (to say through my judges and through my law is to say but one thing).

He took the rather unusual step of ordering his bishops to exercise their authority to punish those they found not following *"the true weye of vertue and good lyving to the pernicious example of othre & lothsomnesse of every wele disposed personne"*. It may be objected that in this Richard was playing the part of hypocrite, since he had fathered at least two illegitimate children. Though this is true, it may be claimed in his defence that his sexual misdemeanours had been committed in the days of his youth and that there is no evidence to show he was anything but completely devoted and loyal to his wife once he married.

Initially, it is possible that Richard had settled the succession on Clarence's son, Edward, the Earl of Warwick, after the death of his son, but later changed his mind, favouring his nephew, the Earl of Lincoln, maybe on the grounds that Edward was mentally unfit to rule. In any case, Lincoln had been made Lieutenant of Ireland, a post which for the Yorkists indicated the heir apparent, equivalent to being the Prince of Wales today. Once more, there is no indication of Richard's motives. It has been harshly claimed that Richard at first created the unsuitable Edward as his heir to forestall any attempt to remove him from the throne. Yet, as all knew that the provision of a weak and incapable heir might simply strengthen Henry Tudor's hand, this is unlikely. It is also claimed, as the threat of Henry Tudor's invasion increased, that necessity dictated a more suitable heir be found. However, there is no evidence for this assertion either.

The case of William Collingbourne shows how a distorted presentation of facts could be employed in order to portray Richard as a tyrant. According to Fabian, Collingbourne was cruelly treated mainly on account of a rhyme.[5]

> *[He] was cast for sondry treasons: & for a ryme which was layde to his charge that he shulde make in derysion of the kynge and his counsayll, as folowith:*
>
> *The catte, ratte, and Louell our dogge*
> *Rulyth all Englande vnder a hogge.*
>
> *The which was meant that Catisby Ratclyffe and lorde Louell ruled the lande under the kynge, which bare the whyte bore for his conysaunce. For the whiche and other… [offences] he was put to the moost cruell deth at the Tower Hylle, where for hym, were made a newe payer of galowes. Upon the whiche, after he hadde hangyd a shorte season, he was cutte down, beynge alyue, & his bowellys rypped out of his bely and cast into the fyre there by hym, and lyued tyll the bowcher put his hand into the bulke of his body; insomuch that he sayd in the same instant, "O Lorde Ihesu, yet more trowble," & so dyed to the great compassion of moche people.*

It interesting that Fabian passes quickly over the most important offences on Collingbourne's part, *"sundry treasons"*, while stressing (and unnecessarily quoting) the mocking rhyme, and thus making it seem that he was executed more for his mockery than his treason. He also seeks to make the reader pity Collingbourne by giving a detailed account of his method of execution and the supposed reaction of the crowd. Thus, in one short section, Fabian achieves at least four things: he makes Richard appear vicious and unbalanced; he can repeat Collingbourne's mockery; he gains sympathy for one who was in fact a traitor; and he can describe how people reacted against Richard's cruelty. The success of Fabian's account can be measured by the comment of Gairdner, an important and influential historian, who maintained a bias against Richard and completely avoided mention of Collingbourne's treason.

> *Colyngbourne, a Wiltshire gentleman, who seems to have been one of the first promoters of Richmond's attempted invasion the year before, suffered the hideous death of a traitor on Tower Hill, not more, it was thought, for that than a well-known rhyme aimed at the king and his three leading councillors.*

Richard also faced severe problems in foreign policy. From what we can glean about his character, it seems likely that it was unsuited to the subtleties and diplomacy needed to conduct such affairs and that he lacked a seasoned adviser. As mentioned earlier, Richard had refused to send troops to support Duke Francis of Brittany in his continuing conflict with Louis XI of France, probably because of his reluctance to become embroiled in the affairs of other countries when he was trying to establish himself as king in his own country. He might have persuaded Francis to hand over Henry Tudor as the price of military support, thus removing a persistent threat. He refused this support and the result was that Francis assisted Henry in his unsuccessful invasion. This stung Richard into action and he began a sea campaign against Breton shipping.

Events on the continent began to complicate matters. The unstable political situation in Brittany made it difficult to formulate a coherent policy. Finally, a truce was signed with Brittany in which Richard agreed to supply most of the archers Francis had originally requested, in return for arresting Henry Tudor. In September 1484, however, being informed of the plan, probably by Morton, Henry engineered his escape and, on the pretext of visiting an acquaintance, fled in the disguise of a servant across the border into France. Commines puts a careful gloss on Henry's flight.[6]

> *Being returned into Bretagne, he was afraid, having 500 English in his train, of becoming burdensome to the duke, and feared he might thereby induce him to make some agreement with King Richard, to his prejudice and disadvantage, for he had some intimation that there were secret practices on foot to that purpose; and therefore, he and his whole retinue went away privately, without taking leave of the duke.*

Once in France, Henry found willing support for his cause.

Vergil's account makes for more exciting reading.[7] He relates that, having been warned by Morton of Richard's intentions, Henry heeded his advice and planned to escape from Brittany into France. He arranged for some of his supporters, under the pretext of sending them to the Duke of Brittany who was near the French border, to ride into Anjou. Henry himself, accompanied by five servants made pretence of visiting a friend living in a town containing many English residents so that suspicions would not be raised. However, after journeying five miles, he changed his apparel for that of one of his servants and rode hard to the borders of Anjou. Riders dispatched with all haste by Peter Landofe, treasurer to the Duke of Brittany and no friend to the English exiles, almost caught him. Meanwhile, the Englishmen remaining in Brittany, who had not been apprised of Henry's scheme, felt fearful and vulnerable, but luckily for them the Duke sent them after Henry, much to Henry's delight.

Louis XI having died, the government of France fell to Anne of Beaujeau, who ruled as regent for her brother, Charles VIII. Her instincts were anti-English, fearing in particular an English invasion. However, the conflict with the Duke of Orleans prevented Anne's immediate focus on Henry Tudor and the English problem. Then, at the beginning of

1485, the Duke of Orleans, having raised a rebellion without the support of Brittany and England, was defeated, thus opening the way for France to provide increased and more effective support for Henry Tudor.

Meanwhile in England Richard had already embarked on a series of measures to court the allegiance of the Lancastrians and the Woodvilles. In August he had arranged for Henry VI's body to be transferred from the relatively unimportant location of Chertsey to the far more prestigious Royal Chapel of St George's at Windsor, the same location as the tomb of Edward IV. It is possible that Richard, who seems to have been genuinely pious, sought to distance himself from the reign of his brother, who had lived his last years indulging his appetites, with a demonstration of his commitment to the memory of Henry VI, who was beginning to be thought of in some circles as a saint, perhaps also in the hope of winning over some of the Lancastrians. In addition, Richard also began to give financial support to King's College, Cambridge, Henry's foundation. By these means he attempted to portray himself, rather than Henry Tudor, as the true successor to Henry VI. The daughters of Elizabeth Woodville, sent out of sanctuary on the strength of Richard's promises, were courteously received at court at Christmas 1484.

It has been asserted on the evidence of Vergil and the Croyland chronicler that Richard began to think about marriage to his niece, Elizabeth.[8]

> *Oh God! Why should we any longer dwell on this subject, multiplying our recital of things so distasteful, so numerous that they can hardly be reckoned, and so pernicious in their example that we ought not so much as suggest them to minds of the perfidious. So too, with many other things which are not written in this book, and of which I grieve to speak; although the fact ought to be concealed that, during this feast of the Nativity, far too much attention was given to dancing and gaiety, and vain changes of apparel presented to queen Anne and the lady Elizabeth, the eldest daughter of the late king, being of similar colour and shape; a thing that caused the people to murmur and the nobles and prelates greatly to wonder thereat; while it was said by many that the king was bent either on the anticipated*

> death of the queen taking place, or else, by means of a divorce, for which he supposed he had quite sufficient grounds, on contracting a marriage with the said Elizabeth. For it appeared that in no other way could his kingly power be established, or the hopes of his rival be put an end to.

This passage deserves some consideration. One can but admire the chronicler's mastery of rhetoric. He begins with dramatic plea to the Almighty and a claim, that Richard's actions are almost too great to relate lest they be heard by the *"perfidious"*. After this calculated appeal to his readers' curiosity he then goes on to write about these dreadful things. It would not have escaped those, well versed in the Sacred Scripture, that the phrase *"many other things which are not written in this book"* is a reference to some words of St John's Gospel, meant to emphasise how far from godly ways Richard had strayed. Again, after writing that a *"fact ought to be concealed"*, he relates it with evident relish. Then he endeavours to find things to condemn in the festivities and the behaviour of the Queen and Lady Elizabeth swapping clothing. Bizarrely, he uses this evidence to suggest obliquely that this indicated Richard's desire for the death of, or divorce from, the Queen, and his wish to marry Elizabeth. It is clear that, after giving a reminder of Richard's supposed wickedness, the writer squeezes and strains to find every possible negative inference.

However, as with all the most important questions about Richard and his reign, it is very difficult to arrive at the truth of Richard's intentions towards his niece. The rumour as recorded in the Mercers' Company Records was that *"the queen was poisoned by consent and will of the king so that he might marry and have to wife the lady Elizabeth"*.[9] But this is almost certainly untrue; Anne died of natural causes in March 1485, having been ill for some time. Yet, the rumours persisted, suspicion no doubt fuelled by the understanding expressed by the Croyland chronicler that such a marriage would strengthen Richard's position in uniting himself with the Woodvilles, so weakening Henry's; and given how Richard had seemingly courted the Lancastrians and Woodvilles, it is not impossible that Richard had thought about such a match; but that is to place conjecture above the evidence.

Richard disclaimed any such intention and asserted in council, according the Croyland chronicler, that he had never considered it.[10] That he declared this in council and in the great hall in the presence of the mayor, aldermen, many lords and other people can be regarded as evidence both for and against the charge of harbouring the idea. The Croyland chronicler maintains that Richard, after shunning his dying wife, needed much dissuading from this course, but then this is the position to be expected of this writer.

> *The king's purpose and intention of contracting a marriage with his niece Elizabeth being mentioned to some who were opposed thereto, the king was obliged to call a council together, to excuse himself with many words and to assert that such a thing had never once entered his mind. There were some persons, however, present, who very well knew the contrary. Those in especial who were unwilling that this marriage should take place, and to whose opinions the king hardly ever dared offer any opposition, were Sir Richard Ratclyffe and William Catesby, Esquire of his body.*

The chronicler believes that Ratcliffe and Catesby had warned him of the danger of rebellion in the north if it were thought he had murdered the queen, and that twelve doctors of divinity had asserted that the Pope would never allow a dispensation for a marriage of such close relations. If in the marriage of Edward IV and Elizabeth Woodville there had been a foreshadowing of the conditions Anne Boleyn would later demand of Henry VIII, there is also a foreshadowing here of the problems that Henry would encounter in trying to obtain a papal dispensation regarding the marriage.

Richard's reign was to some extent undermined by lack of finance. As king he had never enjoyed the wealth that Edward had apparently accrued, a good portion of this having been stolen by the Woodvilles, while the rebellions and threats of invasion had put further strain on the royal coffers. Therefore, Richard was forced to raise money to counter the threat of Henry Tudor's invasion. It has been said with some justification that this was simply a reintroduction of the hated benevolences, abolished by Richard earlier. In the jaundiced words of the Croyland chronicler they were *"the exactions of King Edward which he himself had condemned in Parliament, only avoiding in every case the word "benevolence", a name detestable in every way. Selected men were sent out...who were by means of prayers and threats, by right and wrong, to scrape up immense sums of money, after examining the archives of the realm, from persons of nearly all conditions."* Technically, these were not benevolences, which were forced gifts, but loans to repaid at some future date, though probably the technicality meant little to those who were subjected to them. The problem of taxation was a fault line running through the English constitution. Since parliament had control over taxation, the king often had to find means to raise substantial sums through exercise of his own power. Edward had resorted to benevolences, Henry VII would rely on the prodding of Morton's infamous fork, as well as illegal and corrupt measures, and Henry VIII would pillage the Church. This fault line would crack asunder during the reign of Charles I and help to create the enmities which led to the Civil War. In reality, Richard had no option but to find the finance to resist Henry Tudor, who was preparing for a second invasion, now backed by France, confirmation of which Richard received by 6 January 1485.

Rumours, even if lacking truth or credibility, can sometimes fatally undermine those enjoying power or exercising authority, as Henry was to discover in the case of Perkin Warbeck, and to a lesser extent of Lambert Simnel. Questions surrounding the fate of the princes and Richard's marital intentions towards his niece had weakened his position. Naturally, such rumours, even if not initiated by the factions opposing Richard, were used to justify opposition to him. The apocryphal response of Harold Macmillan to a journalist enquiring about what was most likely to affect government adversely, *"Events, my dear boy, events"*, seems entirely apposite in the case of Richard. It could be argued that whatever he did following the death of Edward IV was doomed to failure. It is easy with the benefit of hindsight to conclude that if only he had taken different course he would have achieved security and success; but even allowing that the worst charges against him are true, every choice facing him presented peril. Had he not taken charge of the young King Edward at Stony Stratford he would have been defenceless against the ambitious Woodvilles. Even should we allow that the children of Edward were not illegitimate, he would have encountered similar danger had Edward been crowned and begun to rule in his own right, guided by the same Woodvilles. If Hastings had not been executed he ran the increased risk of being seen to be weak and of encouraging further plots. Arguably he should have executed Morton, possibly the most intelligent, devious, skilful and dangerous of enemies; however, the execution of such a high-ranking churchman would have brought problems of its own. If he had not placed loyal northern supporters in positions of power and influence there was every chance of the rebels being able to build opposition relatively unopposed. When faced with invasion, he had little option but to increase taxes or run the risk of being unable to discharge the primary duty of a king, to defend his kingdom. Although he seems to have worked with some vigour to unite the nation and to present himself as a good, fair and efficient ruler, the nature of the factions opposing him permitted him insufficient time for this policy to achieve success. He entered the game with a losing position already set and there was little he could do to alter the outcome, except perhaps for adopting one possible strategy. If Henry could be eliminated, the focus of the immediate threats would be removed, giving him the time to pursue his policy of uniting his kingdom. Richard, realising the inevitability of Henry's invasion, began to make plans to resist. It is quite likely that Richard, a proven commander, brave and skilled in battle, was not dismayed by the prospect of invasion, since it played to his strengths and, moreover, presented the chance of a decisive battle that would, if not take Henry's life, destroy his support and credibility.

-8-

Invasion and the Battle of Bosworth

Shortly after Easter 1485 Richard placed Lord Lovell in Southampton to refit the fleet, ready to keep watch on all the southern harbours so that, should Henry attempt a landing in that part of the country, he could unite all the local forces to oppose him. The Croyland chronicler thought that this strengthening of the south was the result of an error, a misunderstanding that Henry was expected to land at a place called Milford near Southampton, rather than at Milford Haven.[1] However, even had Richard received intelligence of Henry's intention to land at Milford Haven he would have been guilty of serious negligence had he not made some attempt to strengthen the south, the easiest and most obvious destination for an invasion force led by Henry. With the benefit of knowing that the invasion had not taken place on the southern coast, the chronicler can smugly assert that *"A great amount of provisions and money was wasted there in consequence of this uncalled for policy"*.

Despite the criticisms at Croyland, Richard was a skilful enough strategist not to commit his forces exclusively to any one part of the country. He established himself at Nottingham, being central enough to counter quickly threats which might appear in any area.

A short while before the invasion, Stanley was allowed to travel to Lancashire, ostensibly to see his family, but Richard being fully aware of his faltering allegiance took Stanley's son, Lord Strange, as a hostage. This was a sensible move, especially since Stanley had some involvement with Buckingham's conspiracy and was married to Henry's mother,

Margaret Beaufort. Indeed, Stanley and his brother had a history of uncertain loyalty and it seems that they preferred to remain uncommitted until the potential victor in any conflict became clear; and if finally forced into any battle they fought half-heartedly. In addition, they had some grievance against the House of York, since they felt that Edward had given Richard power in the north, where they deserved to be favoured. Richard himself had failed to support them in their claim to Hornby Castle, though he had favoured Stanley with land and honours and had fought with him in Scotland. The Croyland chronicler gives an account of the treacherous behaviour of the Stanleys when Richard ordered him to make haste to Nottingham [2]

> *[Stanley] made an excuse that he was suffering from an attack of the sweating sickness, and could not possibly come. His son, however, who had secretly prepared to desert from the king, was detected by a stratagem and taken prisoner; upon which, he discovered a conspiracy which had been entered into by himself and his uncle William Stanley before-mentioned, and Sir John Savage, to go over to the side of the earl of Richmond [Henry]; while at the same time, he implored the king's mercy, and promised that his father would with all speed arrive to the king's assistance.*

Meanwhile, Henry landed at Milford Haven on 7 August, where there was no opposition, with about 4,000 men, at least some of whom were well-trained soldiers, though many were inexperienced, under the command of French officers and the Earl of Oxford - Henry himself having no experience in leading an army to battle - and by 11 August word had reached Richard. The Croyland chronicler wrote that *"On hearing of their arrival, the king rejoiced, or at least seemed to rejoice, writing to his adherents in every quarter that now the long wished-for day had arrived, for him to triumph with ease over so contemptible a faction"*. There is no need to doubt the sincerity of Richard's rejoicing, since, relying on his proven skills in the field, he felt that he would finally be able to remove Henry's threat. He sent letters summoning his forces which gathered at Leicester about 16 August, although there is some doubt about how many of his supporters received these letters. Henry made his way through North Wales relying on his Welsh ancestry to draw more supporters from the principality, some of the chieftains forswearing their allegiance to Richard. With an augmented army of about 5,000-6,000 he then proceeded through Shropshire reaching Stafford on 17 August and Lichfield two days later, where, according to Vergil, he *"was honourably received"*. It seems that while he was at Stafford he held a secret conference with William Stanley, who might have been expected to offer some resistance to his advance.

It is likely that the English nobles wearied by the conflict of the previous years were reluctant to take to the field once more over a claim to the throne. Nevertheless about a quarter of them did field an army for Richard. Among some of his more important supporters were the Duke of Norfolk and Sir Robert Brackenbury; and Richard expected the arrival of Percy, the Earl of Northumberland, whose support was crucial. The accounts of the time tend to exaggerate the size of the forces on both sides and it was certainly not the case as the Croyland chronicler reported that *"On the king's side there was a greater number of fighting men than had ever been seen before on one side, in England"*. Richard's forces, at least in theory, outnumbered Henry's 5,000-6,000 men, but by exactly how far is unclear, especially as it is not possible to determine the exact number of those going over to Henry or refusing to engage in battle. In typically exaggerated style, Vergil claims that Walter Hungerford and Thomas Bourchier defected to Henry and that *"Ther flockyd to him also many other nobole men of warre, who from day to day hatyd king Richard worse than all men lyving"*. It appears that before the day of battle, Henry sent to Stanley to request that he position his forces in line of battle. Unsurprisingly, Stanley refused, preferring rather to wait for the opportune moment to pick the winning side.

Henry almost suffered a catastrophe of his own making. Vergil relates that, being worried about the failure of Stanley to commit himself, Henry *"considering his feare was not for nothing, himself, accompanyd with xx armed men onely, stayed by the way, uncertane what was best as to delyberat what he might do"*, but was then unable to find his army, which meanwhile had moved its position. Finally, he entered a town where he spent the night, anxious lest this misfortune portended disaster, but was so fearful of betrayal he dare not enquire about his army. Fortunately for him he was reunited with the army the following morning.

Vergil presents Richard as being haunted by a terrifying dream on the night before the battle.[3]

> *Yt ys reported that king Rycherd had that night a terryble dreame; foe he thowght in his slepe that he saw horryble ymages as yt wer of evell sprytes haunting evydently abowt him as yt wer before his eyes, and that they wold not let, which vyson trewly dyd not so much stryke into his brest a suddane feare, as replenyshe the same heavy cares: for forthwith after, being troublyd in mynde, his hart gave him theruppon that thevent of the battale following wold be grievous, and he dyd not buckle himself to the conflict with such lyvelyness of corage and countenance as before, which hevynes that yt showld not be sayd he shewyd as appalyd with feare of his enemyes, he reported his dreame to many in the morning.*

It is impossible to say whether or not this report is a true account, though it has the marks of a convenient invention, especially since Vergil uses it to teach a moral lesson, claiming that it was no dream but Richard's guilty conscience afflicting him. But then Vergil distorts his history of Richard generally to show how wicked men suffer the consequences of their evil deeds.

The *Croyland Chronicle* reports the same dream but more believably mentions that such was the confusion in the camp that the chaplains were unprepared to celebrate Mass and that breakfast was also lacking. Nevertheless, it fits the purpose of the chronicler neatly to suggest that Richard went into battle without having prepared himself or his forces spiritually by attending Mass, or physically with food, thus implying an ungodly king who failed to provide for his people. If indeed these were lacking, the most likely explanation is that the Yorkist camp was pressed into action by some manoeuvre on the part of the Lancastrians. The *Croyland Chronicle* then maintains that Richard predicted the ruination of the kingdom whoever won the battle, for, if victorious he would ruin those supporting Henry, while Henry, should he prevail, would do the same for Richard's adherents. Perhaps Richard sent Stanley a final order to draw up his forces with the rest of the royal contingent, if he wished his son, Lord Strange, to live, but received the dismissive reply from Stanley that he had other sons. The Croyland Chronicler writes that in response Richard gave the order to behead Strange, but, whether because there were more pressing matters, or because of the reluctance of those charged with the task, or simply because such an order was never given, Strange survived. That morning a note was found pinned to the Duke of Norfolk's tent warning him of treachery: *"Jocke of Norfolke, be not too bold, for Dickon [Richard] thy master is bought and sold"*.

It is perfectly understandable that a commander may have a sleepless night before a battle; and in Richard's case it is equally understandable that his critics would seek to use this against him by adding their own embellishments.

Among the accounts of the battle Vergil provides the most detailed description, although, since so much concerning Richard is contradictory and confusing, it will come as no surprise that the surviving accounts of the battle are no different. The course of the battle seems to have been generally as follows.

Richard rode out from the Blue Boar Inn in Leicester where he had spent the night, and if he took the most obvious route he would have left through the West Gate and crossed Bow Bridge, the parapet of which according to legend he struck with his spur.

When Henry reached the field of battle he placed his archers under the command of the Earl of Oxford in front of a small number of men, while Gilbert Talbot commanded the right wing, and John Savage the left. Henry followed with one troop of horse and a few footmen, expecting to be reinforced by Thomas Stanley. Henry's right flank was protected by a marsh. The first engagement was between the archers, who, if sufficiently skilled at using the six foot long bow, could fire up to twenty arrows per minute. Then the Earl of Oxford's position came under attack and, relying on his previous battle experience, realised that his men were too far spaced to provide sufficient defence, and so ordered them to close up. In this close formation they attacked Norfolk's forces, who proved reluctant to fight with any great energy, and it was probably during this attack that Richard learned of the death of Norfolk. Percy had refused to engage his forces, probably playing a similar waiting game to the Stanleys. As a last and desperate attempt to turn the course of the battle, Richard, having spied Henry protected by only a small force, gathered some of his men and, pausing only to take a drink at a place named Dickon's Well, in honour of the event, made a charge towards him. In his fierce determination to reach Henry, Richard slew Henry's standard bearer, William Brandon, unhorsed John Cheney, a renowned fighter, and made for Henry himself, but his soldiers withstood the onslaught longer than might have been expected. It seems that it was at this point that William Stanley, who probably also commanded the men of Thomas Stanley, decide to commit his forces, attacking Richard on his left with overwhelming numbers, and so Richard was left fighting alone. Surrounded on all sides, fighting bravely to the last, he was cut down and killed. Recent research, following the exhumation of his skeleton, suggests that among the wounds he received were ten serious enough to leave marks on the bones: an arrowhead lodged in the spine; a glancing blow to the side of the head that sliced off a portion of the bone; a dagger blow to the cheek and cut to the jaw, both of which penetrated to the bone; a chest injury, where the blade penetrated to his ribs; and two potentially fatal injuries, a wound, possibly made by a halberd that pierced the skull and entered the brain, shearing off two flaps of bone on the internal surface of the skull, and a sword stroke that completely sliced off a large section of skull at the back of the head. This effectively marked the end of the battle. Oxford pressed home his advantage and, seeing that all was lost, the remainder of Richard's army fled or surrendered. Henry was crowned by William Stanley on the battlefield with the same crown that Richard had worn into battle, with the words *"Sir, here I make you King of England"*. Yet, even Richard's detractors were moved by his courage and spirit. The Croyland chronicler wrote *"For while fighting , and not in the act of flight, the said king Richard was pierced with numerous deadly wounds, and fell in the field like a brave and most valiant prince."* Rous said that *"he bore himself like a gallant knight and, despite his little body and feeble strength, honourably defended himself to his last breath, shouting again and again that he was betrayed, and crying 'Treason, Treason!'"*, and according to Vergil, *"The report is that King Richard might have sowght to save himself by flight; for they who wer abowt him, seing the soldiers even from the first stroke to lyft up ther weapons feebly and fantlye, and some of them to depart the feild pryvyly, suspected treason, and exhortyd him to flye, yea and whan the matter began manifestly to qwaile, they browght him swift horses; but he, who was not ignorant that the people hatyd him, owt of hope to have any better hap afterward, ys sayd to have awnsweryd that that very day he wold make end ether of warre or lyfe...his corage also hault and fearce, which faylyd him not in the very death, which whan his men forsooke him, he rather yealded to take with the sword, than by fowle flyght to prolong his lyfe, uncertane what death perchance soon after by sicknes or other violence to suffer"*. There is no support for Molinet's assertion that when Richard found himself alone on the field he thought to run after the others, but his horse leapt into a marsh from which it could not extricate itself.

Had either Stanley or Percy engaged on Richard's side, Richard would in all likelihood have prevailed at Bosworth and Henry have been relegated to the margins of English history.

Yet such is the uncertainty over the details of the battle that historians have drawn up varying schemes showing the possible disposition of forces and the course of the battle itself.

Even the traditional location of the battlefield itself has been seriously questioned. There are three locations suggested for the Battle of Bosworth. Traditionally the battle was assumed to have taken place directly to the west of Ambien Hill, though an alternative location is a little to the south west of the same hill. In more recent years the discovery of a number of medieval weapons, cannonballs, armour and a silver badge has provided powerful evidence that the battle took place in a field further south, a little to the west of the village of Stoke Golding. The silver badge depicting a boar and about one and half inches in length was the most significant of the finds, being almost certainly a token given by Richard to one of his supporters who accompanied him in the last fatal charge.

Finally, the victors having completely stripped Richard of his clothing, they laid him across the back of a horse with his arms hanging down on one side, his legs on the other, as though he were hog or wild beast and thus, covered with filth, he was taken back to Leicester with his head banging against the parapet of the same Bow Bridge that he was reported to have knocked against on his way to the battle. At some point, in all likelihood while his body was upon the back of the horse, it was attacked by someone wielding a bladed weapon which pierced his buttocks, marking the pelvis, a detail revealed by the close examination of his skeleton. Presumably this was among the *"the many insults offered"* to his corpse, mentioned by the Croyland chronicler. The body was taken to the church of the Annunciation in Leicester where it was left exposed for two days, probably to prove to the curious that he was truly slain, and was then moved to Greyfriars Abbey where it awaited burial.

On Richard's side Norfolk, Sir Robert Brackenbury, Sir Richard Ratcliffe and Lord Ferrers were slain. Catesby, who was caught later, was executed at Leicester. Henry had enough mercy to allow Catesby to prepare for his death, and he wrote his will, in which appear the enigmatic words *"my lords Stanley, Strange and all that blood help and pray for my soul, for ye have not my body, as I trusted in you"*. It may be that it was Catesby whom Richard charged with killing Stanley's son Lord Strange, but Catesby, for whatever reason, whether from pity for the man or because he thought there was little point in carrying out such an act until it became clear which way the battle was turning, failed to carry out his commission. Thus, he was bitter at the lack of gratitude and support from the ungrateful, self-seeking Stanleys, who, unlike Richard, seeing loyalty as foolishness, preferred a calculating betrayal. Hancock argues a further reason for Catesby's bitterness: that it was Catesby who had allayed Richard's suspicions of Stanley having knowledge of the pre-contract between Edward and Eleanor Butler, thus saving him from being dragged out for execution with Hastings after the council meeting in the Tower.

Henry VII

There is a further mystery concerning Catesby's execution for it seems a little odd, that a lawyer, who probably took no part in the actual fighting, should have been executed, while those who had enthusiastically taken up arms against Henry escaped such a fate. It might be argued that Catesby's death was a consequence of him being the most powerful man in a defeated king's government, yet the opposite might also be argued. If Henry, like kings before him, stood in need of talented men, he could also have benefited from Catesby's experience and obvious ability. There again, it may have been Catesby's knowledge of the pre-contract that explains why he was hunted down after the Battle of Bosworth and executed by Henry, while others who had probably taken more active roles against him were saved from this fate. Political expediency dictated the need to remove the man who could question the legitimacy of Elizabeth of York (Edward IV's daughter) whom Henry, in a gesture symbolising the unity of the Houses of York and Lancaster, intended to marry, strengthening his claim to the throne, with the additional aim of bringing the Wars of the

Roses to an end.

The triumphant Henry proceeded to Leicester where he stayed for two days before making his way to London.

-9-

The King in the Car Park

In the gloom of the church of Greyfriars in Leicester a small group of friars stands in attendance around a hastily dug grave in the chancel before their high altar. This area, the choir, as in all other large religious houses and cathedrals is the private place of worship for the priests, those in religious orders and those assisting them. This is convenient, because this grave and the body lying within it are intended to slip into the dark shadows of time, while a different tale about the man will be created, a tale that will be his enduring legacy. The friars are somewhat apprehensive, as well they might be, for this body that they are preparing to bury is that of a king of England, Richard III. Other cathedrals and abbeys have played host to the mortal remains of kings of England; the friars can recall Edward the Confessor, among others, at Westminster Abbey, Edward II at Gloucester and the previous king, Edward IV at St George's Chapel, Windsor. These dead monarchs have brought increased prestige and wealth to the religious establishments where they now rest, but this burial is different. There will be no prestige or increased revenue from this dead king. Indeed, there is perhaps some unspecified danger in being home to the bones of the legitimate king, defeated by Henry at Bosworth. Even John and Edward II had been given proper burials and impressive tombs. There has not been time to dig a deep grave, so it is fairly shallow and when the body - lacking the dignity of either coffin or shroud, still bearing the filth of the battle field and the indignities inflicted on it by the victorious Lancastrians - is placed in it, it becomes apparent that it is not long enough and the body has to be somewhat folded. The religious rites have been as perfunctory as decency allows. The grave is closed, and the truth concerning the reign of this king who reigned for about two years will be buried too. The tiles are relaid. In ten years' time, when Henry is more confident of his kingdom, the choir of the friary will see a marble and alabaster monument constructed, reminding the friars whose body lies beneath the feet of those celebrating Mass.

The friars would have been justified in entertaining fears about the new House of Tudor, for though the decisive blow was not to be initiated by Henry VII, the rapaciousness of his son Henry VIII would see the destruction of not only this religious house but of all abbeys, monasteries, convents and friaries throughout the land. Despite the turmoil and devastation of the Reformation, the bones of Richard III continued to lie still and quiet, and were even undisturbed by later redevelopments of the site until their discovery in September 2012.

Henry, keen to have Richard's body buried after it had been exposed to public view for all to look upon the defeated king, chose Greyfriars in Leicester, a location that had the advantages of being close enough to the church where the body had first lain so that no long funeral procession attracting embarrassing mourning for Richard was necessary, and of being far enough away from the capital and major centres of population.

Tudor history made his choice of location especially unfortunate for Richard. Greyfriars was dissolved when Henry VII's son, Henry VIII set himself upon the course of destroying all of England's religious houses and it was rumoured that at that time Richard's body had been disinterred and flung into the River Soar, and what purported to be his coffin used as a horse trough. Although this rumour was never universally accepted, the site of Greyfriars was redeveloped several times and the precise location of the church became uncertain. Even if Richard's bones had not been thrown into the river, it seemed that nobody could be sure exactly where they might lie, assuming that they still existed and had not rotted away.

Nevertheless, historians who traced the history of the Greyfriars land following the dissolution, suspected that Richard might have been buried under what had become a car park for council buildings, yet there was such uncertainty about finding the body that it was deemed not to be worth investing time and money in such an excavation. However, the perseverance of Philippa Langley eventually ensured that funds were made available and the excavation began. Her conviction that Richard lay beneath the car park was strengthened by what many would regard as an unscientific hunch, for she reported feeling freezing cold as she passed a particular spot in the car park in 2009. Returning to the car park later, she remarked on the coincidence that in the meantime an *R* (for Reserved) had been painted on the adjacent parking space.

Langley's hunch notwithstanding, the archaeologists conducting the excavations held out little hope of finding Richard's burial place, and so sceptical was Richard Buckley, the archaeologist leading the team, that he said he would *"eat his hat"* if Richard were discovered. Then a skeleton was discovered about a yard away from where the *R* had been painted on the surface of the car park. Fortune had favoured the archaeologists because had the trench been sighted in a slightly different location the skeleton would have been completely missed. From the excavations the archaeologists were able to deduce a great deal about the abbey buildings. Although some parts of the site lie under present buildings, the choir and high altar of the Abbey were found within the car park, and it became clear that the skeleton had been buried within the choir itself, thus heightening expectation that the king had indeed been discovered. However, confirmation of its identity would become available only once the battery of scientific tests was concluded.

The bones were taken to the University of Leicester where the examination of, and tests on, the remains revealed a number of significant findings.

Although the skeleton is gracile and has some female features, it was firmly established as a slightly-built male.

An examination of the teeth suggested that the individual was about 35 years old, while evidence from the bones indicated a man in his thirties. These dates are consistent with Richard's age which was thirty-two at his death. Indicators for his height pointed to anything from 5'3" to 6', although 5'8" would appear to be a likely height.

The bones were subjected to radio carbon dating. Samples of bone were sent to Scottish Universities Environmental Research Centre (SUERC) at the University of Glasgow, and the Oxford Radiocarbon Accelerator Unit, part of the University of Oxford's Research Laboratory for Archaeology and the History of Art. The results initially gave the most probable dates for the burial between 1412 and 1460, which would have been too early for Richard, but analysis of the bones also revealed a diet high in protein, especially seafood, which is consistent with Richard's social status. High protein content has to be taken into account when considering carbon dating results, and the adjusted date suggested that the most likely date of burial lay between 1475 and 1530, which accords with the date of Richard's burial.

The most persuasive evidence that the skeleton is that of Richard III came from DNA testing. In this case mitochondrial DNA was used to establish the connection. Mitochondrial DNA is inherited almost exclusively from the mother. Thus it passes from a mother to her children, but not usually from the father, and so is useful in providing evidence of descent from the female line. The researchers were fortunate to discover Michael Ibsen, a relative of the female line from Cecily Neville, Richard's mother. The discovery of Michael Ibsen at this time was especially fortuitous as males are unable to pass on mitochondrial DNA to their children, and so after him the line will be lost. The tests revealed that the DNA of the bones matched Ibsen's, thus proving that the skeleton discovered in the car park is that of Richard III. A further test on a second DNA line produced the same result.

Richard Buckley attempted to make good his promise by eating a hat-shaped cake.

Much concerning Richard's life, reign and motivation must remain in doubt and will be the subject of continuing controversy, but we now have good evidence for his appearance and physical deformity, and, no longer having to rely solely on portraits of doubtful provenance and accuracy, we have his head and face, scientifically reconstructed from his skull. Something of the lost king at last begins to emerge from the shadows.

The reconstructed face of Richard III

Appendix

An account of the coronation of Richard and Anne

The Coronation of Richard III, A F Sutton and P W Hammond (eds), Gloucester, 1983, pp. 275-282.

The daye and yere aforesaid the King and Queene comynge oute of the Whitehall unto Westminster hall to the Kinges Benche and from thense the King and Queene shall goo upon ray clothe bare foted into Saint Edwardes Shrine and all the noble lordes goinge with him every lorde in his degree as hereafter is writin. From there was going before the King first Trompettes and clarions and then harouldes of armes with the Kinges cote of armour upon theim and after them the Crose with a ruiall procession. First come the prestes with gray ameces then after folowe Abbotes and Byshops with myteres on there heads and their croysys in their handes and the Bishop of Rochester bare the crose before the Cardenall and after them came the Erle of Northumberland with the pointless swourde naked in his hande, and my lord Standly bare the mase of Constableshippe the Erell of Kent bare the secounde swourde on the right hande of the King naked and my lorde Lovell bare the iij swourde on the left hande, than come the Duke of Sufolke with the Septure in his hand and the Erell of Lyncoln bare the crose with the ball, the Erell of Surray bare the iiij swurde of Estae before the King in the skabarde, then came the Duke of Norfolk bearing the Kinges crowne by twine of his handes and anone after him came Kinge Richard the iij in his robes of purpill velvet and over his hede a clothe of Estate the barons of the V portes did it beare and on every stde of the King a bishop going, the Byshop of Bathe and the Byshop of Durham then comme the Duke of Bokyngham bearing the Kinges trayne with a white staf in his hande as highe Steward of England than came before the Queene boeth erelles and barons. The Erell of Hontingdon bare the Queenes septre, the Lord Vicont Lisle bare the rodde with the doffe (dove) and the Erell of Wilsher bare the

Quenes crowne before her. Then comme the Queene between ij busshops in hir robes of a swtte like the Kinges and over hir hede a clothe of estate borne by the barons of the V portes and on every corner of the said clothe a bell of golde and on her head a rych serkelet (circlet) of gold with many preciouse perles and stones sett therin, and my lady of Richemond heyre to the Duk of Someret bare the Queenes trayne, and than comme after theim the Duchess of Suffolk in her robes of estate and on her hede a cronell of golde and then came the Duches of Norfolke lykewyse with other ladyes to the nombre of xx, and after them came boeth knightes and squires and many typstawes (tipstaves) and so they went fowrthe of the pallyce into the churche of the westende and so until they comme unto Saint Edwardes Shrine to the seates of estate, and anone the King and Queen satt downe in their seates and anone as this was done there came up before the Kinge and Queene bothe priestes and clerkes singing the Leten and other priksong with greate realitie ands anone as that was done the King and Queene came down to the high Alter and there they hade greate observance and service and in the meane while the King and Queen departed from their robes and stode naked from the middle upwarde and anone the bishops anointed boethe the King and Queene, and after that this was done the King and Queene changed their robes into clothe of gold and than the Cardenall of Caunterburye and all the byshopes crowned boeth the King and Queene with greate solempnite and anone they sang Te Deum and the organs went and the Cardenall sensed the King and Queene and anone they put on the King Seinte Edwardes Coppe and the bishops toke the Kinge the Septre in his righte hande and the crosse with the ball in his lyfte hande, the Queen bare the sceptere in her ryght hand and the rodde with the dowve in her left hand and when that was done the Cardenall went to the masse and the King and Queene went to their settes again, and anon come up before the King two bishops and kneled with theyre croiseres in there handes downe before him a litill while and so they arose and went and kiste the Kinge one after a nother, and when they hade done so anone they stode beside the Kinge than came up the Duke of

Bokingham and stode on the right hande of the Kinge and the Duk of Norfolke stonding on the lefte side and before the Kinge the Erell of Surrey with a swourd in his hande and there standing all the masse tyme, and on every side of the Quene standing all the masses tyme, the Bishop of Exeter and the Bishop of Norwich and on ether side a ladye knelinge and on the righte hande of the Quene sitting the Duches of Suffolke in her estate and on the left side of the Queene sytting my lady of Richemonde. Then kneling behinde the Queenes fete the Duches of Norfolke with other ladys kneling with her, and so they satte still until the paxe was geven, and whan it was geven anon the King and Queene came downe from their seattes unto the highe aulter and there kneling anon the Cardenall terned him aboute with the holye Sacrament betwixte his hondes and there he departed the oste betwine the Kinge and Queene and so the King and the Queene went up into Saint Edwardes Shrine, and there the Kinge offered and lefte Saint Edwardes Crowne with many reliques and after that the lordes sett the Kinges owne Crowne upon his hede and so the king and the lordes retorne home warde every lorde in his degree according save only these pointes. The King bare the cross with the ball in his righte hande and the sceptre in his lyfte hande, and the Duke of Norfolke bare the cape (cap) of maintenaunce before the King and the Queene bare tye sceptre in her right hande and the rode (rod) with the dove in her lefte honed and these bene the deverseties and so they went forthe until the tyme they comme unto the highe deske at Westmynster halle, and when they were come thether anone the kinge and the Queene toke their chambers and the clothes of estate left still in the hale and in the meane while that the King and the Queene were in their chambers came riding in to the halle the Duke of Norfolke as Erle marshall and his horse traped in clothe of golde downe to the grounde and so he rode aboute voiding the people saving only the kinges servaunts and the Duke of Bokingham and anone the Duke of Norfolke called unto him the marshall saing unto him that the King woulde have his lordes to sitt downe at iiij bordes in the great hall, and at iiij of the cloke the King and the Queen came unto the highe desk, and there the Kinge satt downe to his diner in the middes of the bowdre, and so on the lefte hande of the Kinge setting the Queen nighe hande to the bordes ende and on the right hande of the Queene stode my lady of Surrey, and on the lefte hand my lady of Nothingham holding the clothe of pleasance or estate over her hede when she did eate and drinke and on the right hande of the King sytting the Byshop of Durham in the Cardenalles stede and anone the lordes and ladyes avoided down in the hale and wear sett every lorde in his degree and my lady Suffolk setting in her estate and the Duches of Norfolke and my lady of Richmonde at a nother messe and so for the all the ladyes at a borde syttyng all upon one side in the middle of the hall and at a nother borde sitting the Chancelar of England with other diverse bishops sitting with him and at the seconde borde satt the erelles and at the barons borde sitting the judges and other certein worshipfull men of the lawe the Lord Mayre sate at the table next the Cubborde the barrons of the portes sate at the table behind the lordes anone every man avoided down into the hale and were sett every man to his degree and anone after came in the first course before the King and for the dresser the Duke of Norfolke Erle Marshall of England, Controller Sir Thomas Percy, Treasorer Sir William Hoppton, Chambrelein my lord Lovell, Steward my lorde of Surrye, with a whyte staffe in his hand and master Fywater Sewer ans coming for the the first cowrse one dishe of goulde and another of silver so the Kinge was served all with covered messe and my Lorde of Awdlye Karver unto the King and my Lord Scrope Copbearer, and my Lord Maior of London kepte the Kinges cobarde (cupboard) and when dinner was endyd served the King with a cope of silver and gilte or golde with sweet wyne and the Quene with another and when he hade done he toke the cope for his labor, and my lorde Lovell stode before the King all the diner tyem, and ij Squiers for the bodye leing under the borde all the diner at the Kinges fete, and my lorde Scrope of Upsale Copeberer then the Quene being served in gylte plate and the Bishop Durham served also in sylver all iij with covered mese and at the second course came riding into the hale the Kinges Champion Sir Robert Dimmoke and his horse traped with white silke and redde *downe to the grounde and so he come riding before the Kinge making his obeisance, and anone torned him aboute and an heralde proclaymed declaring in all the halle if there be any man that will saye the contrary why that King Richarde shulde not pretend and have the crowne, and anone every man helde their peace for a while and when he hade all said all the hale cried King Richard and anone as they hade so said the Champion cast down his gauntlet and so he dide thrise in the hale ones before the King and ons in the mydes of the hale and another tyme in the hale dore, and so he returned up again before the King making his obbaycans, and anone one of the lordes brought him a cope wythe wine coverid, and so he toke it in his hande and dranke, and whan he hade done he cast owte the remnant of the wyne and covered the cope again and torned his horse and rode thoroughe the hall with th cupe in his right hande and that he hade for his labor. Then after this come before the King xviij haroles out of a stage in the stage in the hall and iiij of theim wore crownes and anone one of them spake certein wordes unto the King proclaiming his style and when they hade done anone the remnant cried King alarges and so they did iij tymes in the hale and went to their standing again and as to the thirde course it was so lat that there might no service be servide of the same only wafers and Ipocrase and anone after this come into the hale grete lightes of waxe torches and torchetes and when they were comme into the hale anone the lordes arose up and went unto the King making there obeisance and when this was done anone the King and Quyne rose up from the bourd and whent unto their chambers and anone all the people departed and went their wais.*

Notes

Chapter 3

1. W Gregory, 'Chronicle of London', in *The Historical Collections of a Citizen of London in the Fifteenth Century*, J. Gairdiner (ed), Camden Society, 1876, pp. 206-207.
2. *Paston Letters*, J Gairdiner (ed), Vol 1, London, 1872, p. 525.
3. For example, *The English Chronicle* and *Benet's Chronicle*.
4. *Ingulph's Chronicle of the Abbey of Croyland*, H T Riley (trans), London, 1908, pp. 421-423.
5. Quoted in P W Hammond, A F Sutton, *Richard III The Road to Bosworth Field*, 1985, p. 27.
6. Corporation of London Records Office, Journal 6, f. 54 (photograph 488), quoted in *The Road to Bosworth Field*, p. 29.
7. R Warner, *Antiquities Culinariae*, London, 1837, pp. 94-96, quoted in *The Road to Bosworth Field*, p. 31.
8. R Fabyan,, *The New Chronicles of England and France*, Henry Ellis (ed.), London, 1811, p. 654.
9. *The Road to Bosworth Field*, p. 33.
10. Jean de Waurin, *Anchiennes Chroniques* d'Engleterre, E Dupont (ed), Vol 3 (1863), p. 184, quoted in A J Pollard, *Richard III and the Princes in the Tower*, Stroud, 1991, p. 43.
11. P M Kendall, *Richard III*, London, 1955.
12. Quoted in A Cheetham, *The Life and Times of Richard III*, Golborne, 1972, p. 60.
13. ibid., pp. 68-69. A shorter account is to be found in *Fabyan*, p. 660.
14. *Polydore Vergil's English History*, H Ellis (ed), London, 1844, p. 152.
15. *John Warkworth's Chronicle*, J O Halliwell (ed), The Camden Society, London, 1838, p. 18.
16. *The Historie of the Arrivall of Edward IV*.
17. ibid.
18. *The Annals of Tewkesbury Abbey*, K Dockray, *Richard III: A Source Book*, Stroud, 1997, p. 18.
19. C L Kingsford (ed), *Chronicles of London*, 'Vitellius A XVI', Oxford, 1905, p.184

20. *The Historie of the Arrivall of Edward IV.*
21. *Warkworth Chronicle*, p. 21.
22. *Fabyan*, p. 662.
23. T More, *The history of king Richard the thirde,* J R Lumby (ed), Cambridge, 1883, p. 6.
24. *The Calendar of Patent Rolls*, 1467-1477, p. 266, quoted in *The Road to Bosworth Field*, p. 55.
25. *Croyland Chronicle*, p. 470.
26. Chancery Patent Rolls, quoted in Dockray, p. 26.
27. M A Hicks, 'The Last Days of Elizabeth, Countess of Oxford', *English Historical Review*, CIII , 1988, p. 91.
28. Chancery Patent Rolls, quoted in Dockray, p. 33.
29. ibid.
30. York Civic Records, Vol. 1, quoted in Dockray, p. 36.
31. Chancery Patent Rolls, quoted in Dockray, p. 33
32. *Richard III and the Princes in the Tower*, p. 78.
33. A J Pollard, Richard, the North and the Historians, http://www.richardiii.net/2_3_0_riii_leadership.php#governor, 1 July, 2013.
34. York Civic Records, Vol. 1, quoted in Dockray, p. 36.
35. *Richard III and the Princes in the Tower*, p. 74.
36. P. Commines, *The Memoirs of Philip de Commines*, Vol 1, London, 1911, p. 277.
37. *Croyland Chronicle*, p. 478.
38. Quoted in Dockray, pp. 26-27.
39. ibid., p. 27.
40. ibid., pp. 26-27.
41. More, pp. 6-7
42. Vergil, p. 168.
43. *Croyland Chronicle*, pp. 480-481.
44. Vergil. pp. 170-171.
45. Quoted in *The Road to Bosworth Field*, pp. 86-87.

Chapter 4

1. Rous, *History of the Kings of England* , quoted in Hanham, *Richard III and his Early Historians*, pp. 12-1, 123.
2. *Rous Roll*, cap. 63.
3. More, pp.5-6.

4. Vergil, pp. 226-227.
5. *The Great Chronicle of London*, p.278, quoted in Dockray, p. 125.
6. Quoted in A J Pollard (ed), *The North of England in the Age of Richard III*, pp. 193-195.
7. H Walpole, *Historic Doubts on the Life and Reign of King Richard III*, 1768, p. 102.
8. K R Dockray, *Richard III* (Headstart History Pamphlet), 1992, p. 14.
9. A Hanham, *Richard and His Early Historians 1483-1535*, Oxford, 1975, p. 50.

Chapter 5

1. Quoted from Cersei Lannister in George R R Martin's series of novels *Game of Thrones*, which series was partly inspired by the Wars of Roses.
2. *Croyland Chronicle*, p. 436
3. D Mancini, *The Usurpation of Richard III*, quoted in *The Road to Bosworth Field*, p. 95.
4. *Croyland Chronicle*, p. 485.
5. ibid.
6. Quoted in *The Road to Bosworth Field*, pp. 95-97.
7. Quoted in Dockray, p. 44.
8. Quoted in J Potter, *Good King Richard?*, London, 1983, p. 91.
9. *Croyland Chronicle*, p. 487.
10. Quoted in Dockray, p. 56.
11. *Croyland Chronicle*, p.487.
12. Commines, pp. 395-396.
13. R Firth Green, 'Historical Notes of a London Citizen 1483-8', *English Historical Review*, Vol 96, 1981, p. 588, quoted in *The Road to Bosworth Field*, p. 105.
14. Mancini quoted in *The Road to Bosworth Field*, p. 106.
15. *Croyland Chronicle*, p. 488.
16. *The Great Chronicle of London*, pp. 230-231, quoted in Dockray, p. 53.
17. More, pp. 45-48
18. W Shakespeare, *Julius Caesar*, Act 2 Scene 1.
19. P A Hancock, *Richard III and the Murder in the Tower*, Stroud, 2011.

20. *Croyland Chronicle*, p. 488.
21. Quoted in Dockray, p. 50.
22. Quoted in Dockray, p. 53.
23. More, p.63.
24. ibid.
25. Vergil, pp.183-185.
26. Quoted in *The Road to Bosworth Field*, p. 108.
27. R Grafton, *A History of the Reigns of Edward IV, etc* , H Ellis (ed), London, 1812, p. 113, quoted in *The Road to Bosworth Field*, p. 114)

Chapter 6

1. Harleian MS vol 2, pp. 82-83.
2. *Bedern College Statute Book,* York Minster Library, p. 48, quoted in *The Road to Bosworth Field*, p. 140.
3. *Croyland Chronicle*, p. 490.
4. Vergil, p. 190.
5. More, p .82.
6. ibid., p. 84.
7. Vergil, pp.187-189
8. A Wroe, *Perkin*, 2004.
9. Mancini, p. 93, quoted in Dockray, p. 77.
10. Rous, quoted in Dockray, p..79.
11. *Chronicles of London*, Vitellius A XVI, C L Kingsford (ed), Oxford, 1905, p. 191.
12. 'Historical Notes of a London Citizen', *English Historical Review*, Vol 96, p. 588.
13. Commines, pp.49, 396.
14. P Commynes, *Memoirs, The Reign of Louis XI 1461-83*, M Jones (trans), London, 1972, p.397
15. Diego de Valera to the Catholic Monarchs of Castile and Aragon, 1 March 1486, Tudor-Craig, Richard III, p. 68, quoted in Dockray, p. 78.
16. Quoted in Dockray, p. 79
17. Fabyan, p. 670.
18. Harleian MS 433, vol 2, pp. 2, 211.
19. P Ariès *Centuries of Childhood*, Jonathan Cape, 1962.
20. Vergil, p.192.
21. *Croyland Chronicle*, p. 490.

22. Vergil, pp. 193-194.
23. A Williamson, *The Mystery of the Princes,* Gloucester, 1981.
24. More, p. 88.
25. Public Record Office C81/1392/6, transcript by R C and P B Hairsine, quoted in *The Road to Bosworth Field*, p. 145.
26. *Croyland Chronicle*, p. 439.
27. ibid., pp. 495-496.

Chapter 7

1. Vergil, pp. 191-192.
2. Harleian MS 433, Vol. 1, p. 269, quoted in *The Road to Bosworth Field*, p. 165.
3. British Library Cottonian Manuscript Faustina, C.iii, f. 405, quoted in *Annals of Cambridge,* vol. 1, pp. 228-229, quoted in *The Road to Bosworth Field*, p. 145.
4. *Croyland Chronicle*, pp. 496 -497.
5. Fabyan, p. 672.
6. Commines, p. 397.
7. Vergil, pp. 206-209.
8. *Croyland Chronicle*, pp. 498-499.
9. 'Mercers' Company Records, 1485', *English Historical Documents 1327-1485,* A.R. Myers (ed), p. 342.
10. *Croyland Chronicle*, p. 499.

Chapter 8

1. *Croyland Chronicle*, p. 500.
2. ibid., pp. 501-502.
3. Vergil, p. 221.

Select Bibliography

Ashdown-Hill J, *The Last Days of Richard III*. 2011.
Commines P, *The Memoirs of Philip de Commines*. Vol. 1, London, 1911.
Dockray K, *Richard III, A Source Book*. Stroud, 1997.
Fabyan, *The New Chronicles of England and France*. Ellis H (ed), London, 1811.
Fabyan, *The Great Chronicle of London*. London, Guildhall Library, MS 3313.
Gairdner J, *Richard III*. Cambridge, 1898
Hammond P W and Sutton A F, *Richard III, The Road to Bosworth Field*. 1985.
Hancock P W, *Richard III and the Murder in the Tower*. Stroud, 2011.
Ingulph, *Chronicle of the Abbey of Croyland*. H T Riley (trans), London, 1908.
Kendall P M, *Richard III*. London, 1955.
Kingsford C L (ed), *Chronicles of London*. Oxford, 1905.
Mancini D, *The Usurpation of Richard III*.
Markham C E, *Richard III: His Life & Character*. London, 1906.
More T, *The history of king Richarde te thirde*. Lumby J R (ed), Cambridge, 1883.
Pollard A J, *Richard III and the Princes in the Tower*. Stroud, 1991.
Potter J, *Good King Richard?* London, 1904
Tey J, *The Daughter of Time*. 1951.
Vergil, Polydore, *English History*. Ellis H (ed), London, 1844.
Walpole H, *Historic Doubts on the Life and Reign of King Richard III*. 1768.

Index

Act of Attainder, 132
Albany, Duke of, 63, 64
Alkmaur, 30
Ambien Hill, 167
Anne of Beaujeau, 155
Archbishop Rotherham. See Rotherham, Archbishop of York
Ariès, Philippe
   attitudes to children, 133
Baker, Richard, 3, 73
Barnard Castle, 16, 30, 51, 63, 82
Battle of Barnet, 4, 36
Battle of Bosworth, 165–68
Battle of Ferrybridge, 13
Battle of Mortimer's Cross, 13
Battle of Nancy, 57
Battle of St Albans, the Second, 13
Battle of Tewkesbury, 4, 37–39
Battle of Towton, 4, 13
Battle of Wakefield, 4, 10
Baynard's Castle, 110
Beaufort, Margaret, 113, 132, 140, 151
Beaulieu Abbey, 36, 48
Bedern College Statute Book, 118
Bedford, Duke of, George, 45, 47–48
benevolences, 6, 148, 159
Berwick, 63, 64
Bishop Booth. See Booth, Bishop of Durham
Bishop Langton. See Langton, Bishop of St David's
Bishop Morton. See Morton, Bishop of Ely
Bishop of Durham. See Dudley, Bishop of Durham,
Bishop of Lincoln. See Russell, Bishop of Lincoln
Bishop of London. See Kempe, Bishop of London
Bishop of Rochester. See Russell, Bishop of Rochester
Bishop of Salisbury. See Woodville, Bishop of Salisbury
Bishop Stillington. See Stillington, Bishop of Bath and Wells
Bloody Meadow, 37
Blue Boar
   Leicester, 165
Boleyn, Anne, 158
Booth, Bishop of Durham, 30, 51
Bosworth, 7
Bourchier, Archbishop of Canterbury, 15, 80, 92, 113, 163
Bow Bridge
   Leicester, 165
Brackenbury, Sir Robert, 6, 121, 163, 168
Brackenby, Sir Robert, 145

Brandon, William, 166
Buckingham, Duchess of, 9
Buckingham, Duke of, 1, 86, 89, 99, 102, 106, 109, 114, 123, 139, 141
   death, 142
   execution, 6
   implicated in the murder of the princes, 124
   presents petition urging Richard to accept throne, 110
   rebellion, 136–39, 140–43
   responsibility for the deaths of the princes, 132
   rewarded by Richard, 94, 116, 137
   treason, 126
Buckley, Richard, 173, 174
Burdett, Thomas, 58
Burgundy, 29, 32
Burgundy, Duchess of, Mary, 67
   marriage, 57–58
Burgundy, Duke of, 13, 17, 26, 31, 33, 34, 57
Burton, William, 69
Butler, Eleanor, 96, 103
Cambridge, University of, 150
Camulio, Prospero, 14
Canterbury, 147
Carmeliano, Pietro, 77
Catesby, Sir William, 102, 103, 116, 145, 158, 168
   death, 168–70

Charles I, 159
Charles VIII, 155
Chaucer, 80
Cheney, John, 166
Chertsey, 156
Chronicle of English History, 80
Chronicle of London, 116
church of the Annunciation
   Richard's body, 168
Clarence, Duke of, 4, 27, 97, 106, 117
   admitted to knighthood, 15
   appointed, 15
   created Lord Lieutenant of Ireland by Warwick, 31
   death, 59–61
   disloyalty, 23
   dispute with Richard, 43–47
   flees after rebellion, 28
   growing division with Edward, 57–59
   in the care of Warwick, 15
   invades, 30
   Lieutenant of Ireland, 15
   marriage, 43
   reconciled with Edward after Warwick's rebellion, 34
   thwarted attempt to marry Mary, Duchess of Burgundy, 57–58
   turns against Warwick, 33
Collingbourne, William, 153
Commines, Philippe de, 76, 124
Conyers, Sir John, 51

Council of the North, 151
Count of St Pol, 55
Countess of Desmond, 77
Court of Requests, 148
Coventry, 34
Coverham Abbey, 81
Croyland Chronicle, 11, 27, 46, 58, 64, 76, 87, 98, 99, 104, 119, 123, 132, 136, 142, 144, 150, 157, 158, 159, 161, 162, 163, 164, 167, 168
De Regimine Principum, 80
Destruction of Troy, 80
Dickon's Well, 166
Dighton, John, 121
Dorset, Marquis of, 92, 94
Dudley, Bishop of Durham, 114,
Duke of Orleans, 155
Earl of Warwick
    enters London victorious, 31
Earl Rivers, 5, 58, 84, 87, 89, 91, 94, 116
    death, 115
Edmund of York, 4, 10
Edward III, 140
Edward IV, 4, 13, 28, 108, 125, 146, 151
    Battle of Tewkesbury, 37
    captured by Warwick, 25
    care for younger brothers, 9
    coronation, 15
    death, 67
    death of Henry VI, 40
    defeats Warwick at Battle of Barnet, 36
    flees, 30
    give Richard a command for the inavsion of France, 55
    gives Richard power in the North, 42–43
    growing division with Clarence, 57–59
    illegitimacy, 24–25, 59, 106
    immediate effects of marriage, 18–19
    marriage with Elizabeth, 17
    orders execution of Clarence, 59–61
    provokes Warwick's resentment, 21–23
    re-enters London, 35
    released by Warwick, 25–26
    rewards Richard for his loyalty, 27–28
    Treaty of Piquigny, 55–56
    validity of marriage with Elizabeth, 60, 96–97
Edward of Lancaster, 29, 31, 32, 37, 117
Edward V, 1, 4, 5, 128, 135
    birth, 32
    coronation date set, 87
    death, 6
    illegitimacy, 106
    moved to the Tower, 94
    upbringing, 84
Edward, Earl of Warwick, 129, 152

Edward, Prince of Wales,
   Richard's son, 118
   death, 150
Elizabeth of York, 6, 132, 135, 156, 157
Excavation, Leicester, 1-2, 173–75
Fabian, 17, 34, 40, 76, 126, 153
Fastolf's Palace, 9
Fauconberg, 42
Ferrers, Lord, 168
Forest of Wychwood, 117
Forest, Miles, 121
Fotheringhay, 8
Francis, Duke of Brittany, 140, 154, 155
Gairdner, James, 154
Gaunt, John of, 140
Geoffrey of Monmouth
   History, 80
Glasgow, University of, 174
Gloucester, 37, 117
Grantham, 141
Great Chronicle, 93, 99, 105
Great Chronicle of London, 109, 125
Green, John, 121
Gregory, Philippa, 132
Grey, Sir Richard, 5, 85, 89, 91
   death, 115
Greyfriars, Leicester, 7, 168, 171, 173
Guildford, Edward, 135
Guildhall, The, 109

Hancock, Peter, 97, 103, 168
Hastings, 26
Hastings, Lord, 1, 5, 86, 87, 94, 95, 101, 102, 103
   plans to thwart the Woodvilles, 88
Haute, Richard, 85
Henry IV, 140
Henry Tudor, 1, 3, 6, 7, 32, 120, 121, 123, 126, 134, 135, 136, 138, 139, 141, 143, 146, 150, 151, 153, 154, 155, 156, 159, 166, 170, 172
   claim to the throne, 139
   disaster narrowly avoided, 163
   duplicity in trying to remove destroys copies of *Titulus Regius*, 113
   escape from Brittany, 155
   French support for, 156, 159
   in Brittany, 140
   invasion, 162–63
   Morton's fork, 159
   responsibility for the deaths of the princes, 131
   support for Buckingham, 142
Henry VI, 4, 34, 41, 156
   death, 39
   released by Warwick, 31
Henry VII. *See* Henry Tudor
Henry VIII, 158, 159, 172
Historical Notes of a London Citizen, 124

Holbein, 134
Hornby Castle, 162
Hume, David, 108
Hungerford, Walter, 163
Ibsen, Michael, 174
Illegitimacy of Edward IV, 106
Illegitimacy of the princes, 6, 106
Jasper Tudor, 32
John de la Pole, Earl of Lincoln, 151, 152, 153
Kempe, Bishop of London, 104
Kendall, John, 116
Kenilworth, 25
King's College, Cambridge, 156
Kings Lynn, 30
Knaresborough
   dispute, 51–52
Knight's Tale, The, 80
Langley, Philippa, 2, 173
Langton, Bishop of St David's, 78, 114, 117
Leicester, 7, 142, 162, 170
   Blue Boar Inn, 165
   Bow Bridge, 165
   church of the Annunciation, 168
   Excavation, 1–2
   Greyfriars, 2, 171
   Greyfriars Abbey, 168
   Richard's body brought back, 168
Leslau, Jack
   theory concerning the princes, 134
Liber Specialis Gratiae, 80
Lichfield, 163
Lincoln, 136
Lincolnshire, 28
Lollards, 80
London, 13, 14, 92, 117, 143
Lord Strange, 165, 168
Lord Welles, 28
Lose-Coat Field, 28
Louis XI, 29, 30, 48, 57, 67, 154
   death, 155
   Treaty of Piquigny, 55, 56
Lovell, Viscount, 116, 161
Lucy, Elizabeth, 107
Ludlow, 4, 84
Lynom, Thomas, 104
Mancini, Dominic, 59, 60, 85, 87, 89–91, 92, 98, 104, 109, 123
Margaret of York, 17, 57
   marriage of Mary, Duchess of Burgundy, 57–58
Margaret, of Anjou, Queen, 29, 32, 36, 39
Matilda of Hackenborn, 80
Maximilian of Austria, 58, 67
Metcalfe, Thomas, 116
Middleham, 82
Middleham Castle, 16, 42, 48, 50
Milford Haven, 161
Milford, near Southampton, 161
mitochondrial DNA, 174
More, Thomas, 40, 61, 71, 72, 100, 102, 105, 106, 109, 121,

131, 134, 139
Morton, Bishop of Ely, 5, 50, 72, 101, 104, 137, 138, 139, 159
   flees after failure of Buckingham's rebellion, 142
   plotting with Henry Tudor, 155
Neville, Anne, 4, 17, 29, 44, 157
   death, 151, 157
   marriage with Richard, 45
Neville, Cecily, 8, 9, 72, 107, 174
Neville, George, 14, 25, 34
Neville, Isabel, 44
Neville, John, 30
Neville, Ralph, 54, 97
Norfolk, Duke of, 114, 116, 163, 165, 166
North Wales, 163
Northampton, 5, 89, 92
Nottingham, 7, 118, 161
Nottingham Castle, 25
Oxford, 117
Oxford, Earl of, 49, 165, 166
   invasion, 49
Oxford, University of, 174
Pageant of Richard Beauchamp, The, 76
Parliament
   23rd January 1484, 148
   25th June, 1483, 109, 115
Paston, Sir John, 45
Peasants' Revolt, 134
Penrith, 16

Percy, Henry, Earl of Northumberland, 30, 51, 52–53, 63, 64, 115, 116, 163, 166
Pilkington, Sir John, 54
Plymouth, 142
Pollard, Professor A J, 135
Pontefract, 26, 91, 115
Poppelau, Nicholas von, 76
Prince Richard. *See* Richard, Duke of York
Princes in the Tower
   deaths, 6
   deaths, reactions to, 6
   discovery of skeletons, 127
   illegitimacy, 6, 106
   murder, 121–35
Queens' College, Cambridgee, 150
Quinte Curse Ruffe des fais du Grand Alexandre, 76
Rastell, William, 127
Ratcliffe, Sir Richard, 116, 158, 168
Ravenspur, 34
Reading, 117
Reformation, the, 172
Richard II, 134
Richard III, 29, 39
   a summary of the charges against him, 3–7
   accounts of his character, 69, 70, 71, 73, 77, 78
   Admiral of England at nine, 15

admitted to Order of the Bath, 15
admitted to Order of the Garter, 15
appearance, 69-79, 173-75
appointed Duke of Gloucester, 15
arrives in London, 92
at York, enthronement of George Neville, 16
attempts at reconciliation with Lancastrians, 156
Battle of Bosworth, 165–68
Battle of Bosworth, events before, 165
Battle of Tewkesbury, 37
becomes king, 110
benefits from the death of Clarence, 63
birth, 8
bones, examination of, 173–75
brought to court, 21
Buckingham's rebellion, aftermath, 143
Buckinghan's rebellion, 136–39
callls for reinforcements in London, 97
care for choristers, 82
care for his son, 151
Collingbourne's treason, 153–54
comes to the help of Edward, 26

continuity in government, 94, 116
coronation, 4, 113
council confirms his protectorate, 93
Council of the North established, 151
death of Henry VI, 40
death of his son, 150
death of his wife, 151
dispute with Clarence, 43–47
Duke of Gloucester, 4
education, 20–21
Edward gives him a command for the invasion of France, 55
Edward moved to the Tower, 94
establishes his government, 116
establishes his influence in the North, 51–55
establishes chantries, 82
excavation, 78, 166
execution of Hastings, 98–104
finances, 158–59
follows Edward into exile, 31
foreign policy, 154–56
given land by Edward, 15
given power in the North by Edward, 42–43
in the care of Warwick, 15
insecurity of early years, 8–13
interest in Church music, 83

interest in education, 82
interest in justice, 53–54, 152
invests his son - Prince of
    Wales, 118
legal reforms, 148–49
loyal to Edward, 23
made Protector, 85
marriage with Anne, 45, 47
oath of fealty to Edward V, 86
physical appearance, various
    accounts and portrayals,
    69–79
piety, 79–83, 83
portrait altered, 74
possible first meeting with
    Anne, 17
prepares for invasion, 161
presides over court after
    Battle of Tewkesbury, 37
reaction to Clarence's
    execution, 61
received in London, 93
reconciliation with Elizabeth,
    149–50
responsibility for death of
    Henry VI, 41
responsibility for the deaths
    of the princes, 131
rewarded by Edward, 27–28
rewards Buckingham, 94, 137
royal progress, 117–21
rumours regarding his
    intention to marry his
    niece, 156–58

sent to capture Fauconberg,
    42
Stanleys' disloyalty, 161–62
succession, Earl of Lincoln,
    152
summoned back to England
    by Edward, 14
support for Clarence, 59
support of, and for York, 54
takes Edward V into his care,
    88–91
takes Richard, Duke of York,
    into his care, 104–6
to Utrecht, 13
treatment of dowager
    Duchess of Warwick, 48
Treaty of Piquigny, 56
war with Scotland, 63–66
with Percy in the North, 52–
    53
Richard, 3rd Duke of York, 10
Richard, Duke of York, 5, 91,
    105, 128, 135
River Severn, 142
River Soar, 2, 172
Rivers, Earl, *See* Earl Rivers
Robin of Redesdale, 24, 25
Rochefort, Guillame de, 125
Rocheforts, 125
Rotherham, Archbishop of
    York, 92, 99, 102, 104
Rous, John 48, 60, 70, 85, 117,
    167
Royal College of Physicians, 135

Russell, Bishop of Lincoln, 94, 104, 114, 128
Salisbury, 142
Sandal Castle, 10
Sarum Use, 82
Scotland
   Richard wages war against, 66
Seaham, advowson, 81
Shakespeare, 3, 63, 69, 98, 102
Shaw, Dr Ralph, 106
Sheriff Hutton, 16, 150
Shore, Jane, 101, 104
Shropshire, 163
Siege of Thebes, 80
Simnel, Lambert, 134, 159
Simon, Richard, 134
Somerset, Duke of, 37
Southampton, 161
Southwark, 147
St George's Chapel, Windsor, 102, 156
St John's Gospel, 157
St Martin-le-Grand, 44
St Paul's Cross, 106
Stacey, John, 59
Stafford, 163
Stallworth, Simon, 141
Stanley, Thomas, Earl of Derby, 5, 28, 51, 100, 102, 104, 117, 161, 165
   disloyalty, 162
   grievances against Richard, 162

Stanley, William, 163, 166
   crowns Henry Tudor, 166
Star Chamber, 152
Stillington, Bishop of Bath and Wells, 103, 114
   the precontract, 96–97
Stoke Golding, 168
Stony Stratford, 5, 89
Stow, John, 77
Strange, Lord, 161
Stubbs, John, 133
Swinford, Katherine, 140
Talbot, Gilbert, 165
Tewkesbury, 37, 117
Tewkesbury Abbey, 37, 117
The Hague, 31
Titulus Regius, 110–13
Tower of London, 103, 121, 123, 127
Treaty of Piquigny, 56, 67
Tudor, Owen, 139
Twynho, Ankarette, 59
Tyrell, Sir James, 6, 50, 121, 131, 145
Valera, Diego de, 125
Vaughan, Sir Thomas, 5, 91
   death, 115
Vergil, Polydore, 37, 60, 63, 65, 73, 105, 107, 120, 121, 135, 137, 146, 155, 156, 163, 164
Vitellius, 124
Walpole, Horace, 77
Warbeck, Perkin, 123, 127, 134, 159

Warkworth Chronicle, 40
Warwick, dowager Duchess of, 47, 48
Warwick, Earl of, 4, 13, 15, 29, 32, 36, 80
   alliance with Queen Margaret, 29
   defeated at Battle of Barnet, 36
   disaffection over Edward's marriage, 22
   flees after rebellion, 28
   forced to release Edward, 25–26
   French alliance, 32
   invades, 30
   plots, 24
   rebellion, 24–25
Welles, Sir Robert, 28
Westminster, 91
Westminster Abbey, 113, 127
Westminster Hall, 110
Weymouth, 36
Whitelaw, Archibald, 76
Williamson, Audrey, 139
Windsor, 117
Woodstock, 117
Woodville, Bishop of Salisbury, 5, 85
Woodville, Edward, 144
Woodville, Elizabeth, 17, 58, 59, 101, 104, 105, 116, 136, 144
   gives birth to a son, 32
   influence, 20
   plans to take control of Edward V, 86–87
   release of daughters from sanctuary, 149
   seeks sanctuary again at Westminster, 91
   seeks sanctuary at Westminster, 32
Woodville, Sir Edward, 5, 87, 92
Woodvilles, 28, 59, 67, 84, 87, 113, 116, 136, 141, 149, 157
   press for Clarence's execution, 60
Worcester, 117
Wroe, Ann, 123
Wycliffe, John, 80
York, 16, 34, 97, 118
   support for Richard, 54
York Minster, 86
   college of priests, 81
   Richard's patronage, 81
York Use, 82

Books by the same author

The Medieval Boy Bishops

A fascinating history of a highly popular tradition across Europe where the boys were given a suprising position and power. It is also the the story of violence, civil unrest and even murder.

A Concise History of West Derby (Liverpool)

A concise but lively and interesting history of West Derby, Liverpool, containing some little known facts and the story of the West Derby ghost.

Children's Books

The Twins Win and Win Again (ages 7-9)
The Twins Come out on Top (ages 7-9)
The Three Wishes (ages 9-11)
Kit in Battle (ages 9-12)
Kit in Danger (ages 9-12)
Kit and the Invention (ages 10-13)

Printed in Great Britain
by Amazon